James Alexander is the pen name of a Scottish veterinary surgeon with over 50 years' experience of treating many different kinds of animal. He is most fortunate to have lived through the era when vets had to be omnicompetent in the treatment of all species and at the age of nine to have been inspired by the famous James Herriot who he 'assisted' whilst operating on a piglet on a farm in Yorkshire. He has cared for most species (and their owners!), ranging from farm animals in the Highlands of Scotland to exotic pets and zoo animals.

To my wife, Anne Marie, and family: David, Robert and Helen, with apologies for a frequently interrupted home life.

James Alexander

ANIMAL AND CLIENT ENCOUNTERS

AUSTIN MACAULEY PUBLISHERS™
LONDON • CAMBRIDGE • NEW YORK • SHARJAH

Copyright © James Alexander 2023

The right of James Alexander to be identified as author of this work has been asserted by the author in accordance with sections 77 and 78 of the Copyright, Designs and Patents Act 1988.

All rights reserved. No part of this publication may be reproduced, stored in a retrieval system, or transmitted in any form or by any means, electronic, mechanical, photocopying, recording, or otherwise, without the prior permission of the publishers.

Any person who commits any unauthorised act in relation to this publication may be liable to criminal prosecution and civil claims for damages.

All of the events in this memoir are true to the best of the author's memory. The views expressed in this memoir are solely those of the author.

A CIP catalogue record for this title is available from the British Library.

ISBN 9781035800445 (Paperback)
ISBN 9781035800452 (Hardback)
ISBN 9781035800469 (ePub e-book)

www.austinmacauley.com

First Published 2023
Austin Macauley Publishers Ltd®
1 Canada Square
Canary Wharf
London
E14 5AA

I would like to acknowledge the 'arm-twisting' and encouragement to write my 'stories' by Lisa Marie Hawthorne and Kathy Peebles, without which this book would never have happened! Thank you also to Martin and Elizabeth Harker for their advice and help with proofreading when I was undecided about proceeding to publishing.

Sincere and grateful thanks must also go to the editors and staff at Austin Macauley Publishers for all their invaluable help and assistance in making this book come to fruition.

To all of my former colleagues and to the many, many clients and their animals who I have had the honour of treating and without which there would have been no anecdotes nor adventures to relate! Very many thanks indeed.

Table of Contents

Fluff the Squirrel Saga	11
Tiny	27
Early Morning Call Out	34
It's a Hard Life!	48
Never Underestimate People	66
If Only They Couldn't Talk!	76
End of Life Services	95
Unusual Encounters	108
Equine Encounters	119
Your Life in Their Hands, or in Their Teeth and Claws! Narrow Escapes!	133
House Calls	150
Drowning the Pine Snake!	163
New Beginnings	168
People Skills	178
The Things People Say	191

| Phone Calls and Chinese Whispers | 197 |
| Rapport with Clients! | 205 |

Fluff the Squirrel Saga

"Here, look after this, could you? We've just found it under a tree."

It was more of a demand than a question, as a shoebox was pushed over the desktop towards the receptionist. Without a please or thank you, the box deliverer quickly exited the surgery! One never knows what is going to be contained within a closed box. Although it is always intriguing investigating the contents. This is done carefully since the occupant may fly, jump or even slither out in an attempt to escape.

There was no sound coming from the box and that is sometimes an ominous sign of either it containing a deceased animal or something that is mute, such as a reptile! A gentle shake elicited no response and so the receptionist took the box through to the nurses' area to see what it contained. All doors and windows were shut in case there might be an escape from the box. It wouldn't have been the first time that the staff had been surprised by the apparent sudden resurrection and subsequent escape into the premises of a supposedly ill or moribund patient!

The lid was carefully raised and the nurses peeped into the box, at the bottom of which reposed a greyish fluffy bundle that was enveloped in a grey fluffy tail. What was it? Was it alive? Just as these deliberations were taking place the furry creature stirred slightly and one little, dark eye opened and blinked. This one eye was just visible as it looked up at the vet nurses in a most cute and appealing manner. They were quite used to getting 'eyed up', but it was normally by some amorous males of their own species!

"Ah it's alive," was the chorus from the assembled nurses, followed by more oohs and aahs and then, almost in unison, "Isn't it just so cute! It's absolutely gorgeous. It's a baby squirrel!"

Loving hands carefully extracted it from the box and it began to move some more and opened both its eyes. The baby squirrel appeared to be thin and a little dehydrated and so no time was lost in preparing some fluids and kitten milk to feed it, and at the same time giving it a nice cosy nest/bed. Veterinary nurses just love looking after any animal that is sick but there is no doubt at all that cute baby animals that need hand rearing are always their favourites. They certainly cause their maternal instincts to kick in. Within a very short space of time, a kitten-feeding bottle with a tiny teat was found and warm kitten-milk was prepared.

Young animals are quite often reluctant to feed from an artificial teat with artificial milk, especially if they are used to being suckled by their mothers. It takes time and patience to not only feed them but also in the early stages of their lives to stimulate them to pass bowel motions and to urinate. Their mothers will lick and clean them after feeding to get them to carry out these functions. However, for some reason, most veterinary nurses tend to stick to using damp cotton wool in order to replicate the action of the mother's tongue!

This small bundle of fluff could potentially present quite a challenge to get to feed since it was now orphaned and had presumably fallen out of a tree.

There were no obvious injuries seen so that was a good start. The nurse who had prepared the milk took the baby squirrel which, by this time, had been getting lots of cuddles from the rest of the staff members and commenced its gentle introduction to hand feeding. She cradled it on its back in the palm of her hand and brought the tiny teat and bottle up to its lips. Would it take any of the milk was the question? She was just getting ready to coax it to feed, when it grabbed the bottle with both hands, lay back and fed itself!

So, there was this little, orphaned baby squirrel feeding itself at the first attempt! Amazing, but most unusual!

It can't have been more than about 2–3 weeks of age and the obvious conclusion was that this baby had not been found recently but that someone had attempted to feed it previously. It seemed to be quite used to human beings and after a good feed it began to move about.

The nurses just loved the baby squirrel and took turns to cuddle and cosset it until I told them that they really had to distance themselves from it so that it didn't become humanised, also in case that it might have a chance of being released back into the wild once more (now an illegal procedure since the Wildlife and Countryside Act 1981).

With great reluctance and heavy hearts, they did their very best to comply with my request and the squirrel was kept away from too much human contact in a large cage.

As many small creatures do, it grew rapidly and soon needed to be moved to another, larger cage so that it could get exercise, running up and down the wires and on the branches that were placed within it. Most of them got pretty chewed up and a steady supply of branches was needed. Any items that were within 'squirrel reach' were rapidly dragged into the cage and reduced to matchwood, including cupboard handles that happened to be just too near!

From being a cuddly cute pet, he had soon grown into a delinquent adolescent animal that was becoming a little bit of a problem to look after. He was growing too big and was becoming too active to keep him incarcerated any longer and so his return from captivity to freedom needed to be urgently arranged.

We were quite proud of the fact that he hadn't been tamed and that he was a suitable candidate to re-join his wild cousins. This turned out to be a bit more difficult than I had anticipated because we didn't know where he had been found, and everywhere that I contacted refused to accept another squirrel on their premises. Our poor little, cute squirrel was even earning a few epithets over the phone such as 'Tree Rat or Grey Vermin'! We hadn't even given him a name since to do so would have been too humanising.

I resolved to just take him away into a country lane and release him into a wood where he could enjoy a happy life filled with happiness and freedom. We duly caught him up, placed him in a carrying cage and with a few fond farewells from the staff, he was loaded into my car.

My last call that afternoon was to visit an unruly Doberman, who belonged to a lovely older couple, who lived in the country. He was called Max but he might as well have been called Mad Max since he was totally untrained and usually careered around the room at, what seemed to me to be, head height! He was a nice enough dog but just a bit of an excitable nutcase and I just knew that it would take ages to catch him.

His owners, Mr and Mrs Gordon, were an extremely sociable and friendly couple and were always very hospitable. Although I liked going to see them, it could be a little bit frustrating if I was in a hurry, not only because of the time taken to catch Max as he continuously circled around the room and constantly dived, at great speed, under and over the furniture but also because Mrs Gordon always had a tea tray set with delicate china tea cups, linen napkins, cucumber sandwiches and ham and asparagus rolls which she insisted that I consumed after Max had been finally caught and examined!

The refreshments were a very kind thought but the serving of the tea was just the prelude to a longish session of chatting which I usually couldn't spare the time to do! My protestations of other calls or urgent things to do were always politely brushed aside by Mrs Gordon.

"Oh, I'm sure that you can spare the time to have a little cup of tea with us. I have made some sandwiches and the kettle is just boiling. I've made some tasty sandwiches especially for you," or, "we are just going to have a little, light 'luncheon'; surely you can join us?"

They were a lovely, retired, professional and well-educated couple. Mrs Gordon had been privately schooled in the Far East, was extremely genteel and mannerly and everything had to be 'just so' and done 'properly' in both her domestic and social life. In many ways, she reminded me of a rather 'posh' television character called 'Hyacinth' and I had the distinct impression that Mrs G knew that I had those thoughts!

Mr Gordon unfortunately had suffered a number of strokes and although he could just about walk, albeit with difficulty, he was unable to speak. Fortunately, he was able to read perfectly and could watch the television. Mrs Gordon loved talking and more than made up for her husband's speech disability and regularly carried out what would have been his side of the conversation as well as her own!

As Mrs Gordon was serving tea, I had a sudden brainwave. I was aware that they owned a huge wood which was at the far end of their immaculate garden.

"I've got a young squirrel in the car," I said to Mrs Gordon. "It is an orphan that we have been hand-rearing in the surgery and it is time for it to be returned to the wild. I was going to let it go somewhere while I was on my way home after this visit, but just suddenly thought that you might let me release it into your wood?"

"Just a minute," was the reply. "I will just ask Arthur," and she turned around to ask him.

Unbeknown to her, Arthur had already raised both his thumbs as an indication that it would be OK.

"Arthur, dear, Mr Alexander has kindly asked us if he can release a baby squirrel into our woods. Would that be, OK?"

Arthur gave another 'thumbs up' sign and attempted to grin. Mrs Gordon then turned back around to face me and said, "Arthur says that it is so extremely kind of you to consider us, and our wood, as a potential home for your squirrel. We will be delighted if you wish to release it here! Go and get it!"

Wow! I inwardly smiled at what had been the somewhat loquacious interpretation of a simple 'thumbs up' sign! At least my release issue had now been solved!

"Do have some more tea and please have some more sandwiches, I have made them especially for you." It was often more like an order than a request!

However, after I felt that I had done justice to the feast, I suggested that I went and got the squirrel from my car. I brought the squirrel into the house in its travelling cage and showed it to them.

"Aw, Arthur, isn't he just so cute? Look at his furry tail! How old is he? Has he got a name? I know, we will call him Fluff!"

I had no idea whether 'Fluff' was male or female but he/she definitely now had a name!

"Where will we release Fluff?" she said, "I know, we will release him on the back lawn which is surrounded by trees and he can make his way into the wood from there. Oh, isn't this exciting?"

Mrs Gordon led the way through the rear door of the house into the rose garden and across her manicured lawn where she stopped.

"Isn't it a wonderful warm, sunny day? Let us release Fluff here. Oh! Isn't he lovely? He is just so cute!"

I opened the basket and Fluff leapt out onto the lawn. He had never felt grass below his feet before, and most certainly not a newly mowed lawn. With a leap into the air, he happily zig zagged across the lawn towards the trees. One could almost imagine him whooping with delight. I gave an inward sigh of relief since I could now see an end to my squirrel problem. Little did I know at that point that the squirrel problems were just beginning!

As I stood next to Mrs Gordon, who was attired in a loose summer frock, I noticed that Fluff had decided to take a detour and instead of heading for the nearest tree, it veered off course towards a metal clothes pole. Promptly and with surprising agility he shot up it, right to the very top. I was just beginning to wonder whether he knew what a tree actually was, since he had never been outside before, when I saw that he was coming down the pole at a faster speed than he had gone up it. Was he going to head for the woods now?

As he hit the ground he commenced running at top speed across the lawn, again in a zigzag fashion, but this time instead of heading for the trees it became quite clear that he was heading straight towards us! Without even pausing he appeared to bump into Mrs Gordon's ankles. She promptly let out a somewhat embarrassed or maybe excited squeal as he then raced up her legs, under her dress, presumably right to the very top! After emitting another squeak, a gasp, a little giggle and a small jump Mrs Gordon's cheeks flushed bright crimson! She remembered her girls' boarding school days and how to deal with males who were intent on exploring ladies' underwear but she couldn't immediately bring to mind any instructions about how to discourage a squirrel from doing so!

For my part, I couldn't remember any lectures from my time at vet school that gave specific advice on how to retrieve little fluffy animals from between ladies' legs! Fortunately, Fluff, obviously didn't find anything of interest within the summer frock for he reappeared pretty swiftly and ran away across the lawn to disappear into the wood.

Mrs Gordon was still quite flushed and breathing rather heavily. "Oh my!" was all she could say! I shut the basket and started to walk back to the house. It wasn't every day that she got her nether regions investigated by a furry creature! Apart from a little excitement there seemed to be no harm done and I headed home for a rare evening of not being 'on call'.

That very evening, at about 10:30 p.m., I got a phone call from the vet who was on call. He informed me, that he had just received a phone call from an extremely distressed Mrs Gordon because there was a squirrel running about inside her house and she thought that it was Fluff! I was to go out to her house immediately and catch the errant squirrel. The vet told her that I wasn't on duty that night and all that she needed to do was to open her door and let the squirrel out and that he would leave a message for me to telephone her the next day.

The weather had been unusually warm that summer and they surmised that the squirrel had entered the house through one of their open windows. When I telephoned Mrs Gordon the next morning, she related all that had happened and although unhappy that the vet who was on call hadn't attended immediately, she acknowledged that the situation had been resolved satisfactorily but she also lamented upon the fact that they would now need to keep their windows shut for a few days.

All's well that ends well I thought to myself. At least that is the end of the Fluff saga! He must have got lost and a bit disorientated in his new surroundings and ended up inside the house. Little did I know then that it was just the beginning of a Fluff saga!

At our surgery, we employed a cleaner who carried out her work every evening once the consultations etc. were finished for the day. She asked me, "Where has the little squirrel gone?"

I told her that I had released him into a wood and that he was back in the wild and that he now had his freedom.

"Oh no! I will really, really miss him," was her reply, "He was such good fun. I used to let him out every evening when there was nobody here and we played chasing games round the surgery. He would even run up my legs and sit on my shoulder! I'm really sad because he was really becoming quite tame!"

"You did what?" was my astonished question. "We have all been trying to distance ourselves from him for the last few weeks and to keep him wild so that he wouldn't become humanised and now it looks like it has been a complete waste of time!" No wonder the squirrel wasn't afraid of running up Mrs Gordon's dress. That certainly explained a lot of things!

Mrs Gordon duly kept all her windows and doors firmly shut and put up with the stifling heat, even going as far as to keep the storm doors shut together along with her ordinary outside doors. Maximum squirrel defence!

She was busy making Arthur's breakfast of a boiled egg, tea and toast and was just pouring the hot water into the teapot when she heard the noise of her letterbox closing. *The postman's early this morning* she thought to herself and just as she did so, she heard the letterbox closing again. "Oh, how exciting!" was her reaction, "We must be getting two letters today!"

Arthur and Mrs Gordon occupied single beds in the same room and as she carried in the nicely set breakfast tray, she was wondering what the morning post might consist of. How very exciting it would be to get two letters on the same day!

She stepped backwards into the room and pushed the door open with her body and then turned around to greet Arthur with the good news that there were going to be two letters to be opened. She went to put the tray down on the bottom of

Arthur's bed and as she did so she saw Fluff sitting right on the end of his bed with Arthur just looking at him. Remember, of course, that he couldn't speak and hadn't been able to warn his wife that he had a new bed companion! The noises of letter boxes closing had been the squirrel coming in through the front storm door (1st letter!) and then subsequently entering the house through the inner door letterbox (2nd letter!) and then making his way into their bedroom.

When she saw Fluff sitting on the end of her husband's bed, Mrs Gordon screamed and almost dropped the tray that she was carrying. This somewhat startled Fluff, who was only trying to be sociable with his new friends and he launched himself off the bed to a place of safety which just happened to be straight up Mrs Gordon's short summer nightie! I would have loved to have been there to see her face and to hear what she said! I'm pretty certain that it wasn't along the lines of, "Get down out of there you little rascal!"

How long he was up there, I have no idea, I suspect it was only a fleeting visit since he had explored those regions before! Her squeals and wriggles certainly did the trick and he zoomed down her legs, jumped back onto Arthur's bed and then he performed an almighty leap straight onto Arthur's head, where he proceeded to slip and slide on his balding pate!

Once he had regained his footing, Fluff then began, from this high vantage point, to sit up on his haunches and started to wash his face and groom his tail! Mrs Gordon was still suffering from palpitations or shock from once again having been molested by the squirrel while Mr Gordon was in a state of apoplexy due to the squirrel adorning his head! Whatever hand gestures he made at this time, I have no idea of, but I suspect the translation would have been something along the lines of what he had learned in his Royal Navy days. "Get this so and so of a squirrel off my head. Right now!"

This time, Mrs Gordon, despite her degree of excitement and stress, remembered the vet's instructions and so she opened both of the front doors and managed to shoo Fluff out of the house with the napkin off her breakfast tray, while simultaneously holding her nightie between her legs so that her private parts weren't subject to any more uninvited or unexpected morning assaults. Twice in two days was more than enough for a genteel, mature Lady!

Yet again, I had to have another telephone consultation with Mrs Gordon. She was, as always, very polite but was also very direct, expressing her sadness and annoyance at the turn of events because although Fluff was really a very cute squirrel she really couldn't cope with any more adventures. She resolved to keep her windows and doors firmly shut, even though the weather was exceptionally warm and in addition she was going to seal the letter boxes shut with adhesive tape. Hopefully, Fluff would be defeated and discouraged from his endeavours to be sociable with his human friends and would seek more appropriate squirrelly company! *Amen to that*, I thought, for I too was tiring of Fluffs adventures!

The Gordon's lovely house was tastefully furnished with many antique items and expensive ornaments from Mrs Gordon's time spent in the Far East and it was always immaculate. Their social circle had diminished considerably since Arthur had become disabled and they got very few visitors. However, those that still visited were their closest friends and knew the house and its furnishings, and Max, the mad canine, very well.

The next day after the breakfast time episode, Mrs Gordon had a visit from one of her friends. She was too polite to ask why the storm doors were shut on a warm summer's day and as she was being shown into the day room, she happened to glance into the best lounge as she passed the partly open door. *Wow!* she thought, *That looks a bit of a mess! Perhaps Max has been naughty?*

"Has Max been a naughty boy then?" she asked.

"What do you mean? He's out in the garage where he always is when we have visitors. You know how boisterous he is, always leaping over the furniture and knocking things over."

"Well, I couldn't help noticing that your best room looks a little bit, er, well, kind of disturbed," said her friend trying to be diplomatic.

They pushed the door open and then gasped in horror as they surveyed a scene of absolute carnage!

The lounge was a tastefully decorated and furnished room that was rarely used any more since they did little in the way of entertaining now. The three-piece suite, was a light oatmeal colour as were the carpets and matching curtains. A few, tastefully selected, small items of furniture such as coffee tables were arranged around the room as were a couple of standard lamps and some greatly prized Jade ornaments and delicate Indian silverware, brought from the Far East. A tall yucca plant nestled in a corner near the window, Cyclamen plants were arranged on the windowsill, but the focal point of the room was a beautiful open fireplace.

Sadly, that description no longer applied because the standard lamps were lying on the floor along with the yucca plant which had fallen over and the soil in its container had spilled over the carpet. The ornaments and cyclamen plant had been cleared off the surfaces and there were many black and muddy footprints all over the carpet, the oatmeal suite and even up and down the curtains! The windowsill was covered in a mixture of soil, sooty footprints and what look very like poo! What in all the world could have happened? Poor Mrs Gordon was speechless and in a state of shock about what had happened to her best room. The culprit was nowhere to be seen but he had definitely left his squirrel calling card, in fact many of them, on the carpet, on the settee and on the windowsill!

They then spotted a black, fluffed-up apparition which was sitting behind the curtains. Aha! There was the culprit and before he could cause further chaos, with great presence of mind, her friend dashed across the room, opened one of the windows and shooed him out. Once they had both recovered from the shock of seeing the carnage, it began to dawn on them about what had happened. All the doors, letterboxes and windows had been sealed against squirrel entry, but Fluff was more than a match for their anti-squirrel strategy! He had managed to climb onto the roof and like a cross between Father Christmas and an old-fashioned chimney sweeps' brush he descended down the chimney into the best room, efficiently cleaning the chimney of soot with his bushy tail as he did so!

That, of course explained the black and sooty footprints that covered the furnishings. Hoovering up soil and dry soot would have been a bad enough prospect in itself, considering the light colour of the carpet and the curtains, but in his panic to get out of the room Fluff had created a pretty good imitation of Indian Ink by mixing soot and the evacuated contents of his stressed bladder: subsequently tramping through it and redecorating the whole lounge in a black, squirrel's tail and footprint pattern!

Oh dear! Specialist upholstery and carpet cleaners were going to have to be called in to try and sort the mess and a solution would need to be found for the 'Fluff problem'!

I had never heard Mrs Gordon speak with anything other than carefully modulated tones before, even when Max was being a 'little rascal' and refusing to be caught, but as soon as I heard her voice on the phone, I immediately discerned that she was pretty angry!

"You will come down here immediately and catch this squirrel. I have definitely had enough of him!" Then she related the whole story! I felt absolutely awful for her but there was no way that I could possibly have predicted the events that had taken place!

I managed to borrow a trapping cage that was a suitable size to catch a squirrel and then, with a certain amount of trepidation, visited her home. To give her full credit, being the lady that she was, she tried to make light of the events but I could tell that our relationship that day was somewhat strained!

I took the trap and set it up on her lawn near the trees where we had released Fluff and baited it with some tempting morsels of food. Over the course of the next few days, I had successfully trapped a variety of angry blackbirds, magpies and extremely annoyed adult grey squirrels but I never managed to catch Fluff! During this time the weather remained unseasonably hot and the poor Gordons lived in something resembling a sauna since every possibly entrance and exit to the house was now completely and definitely sealed! This, of course included stuffing newspapers up the lounge chimney.

Eventually she relaxed the fortifications and Fluff was never seen again. The only explanation I could think of was that the native squirrels must have had some racialist tendencies and having met the 'sooty black' creature, an interloper 'of colour', he wasn't going to be welcome on their patch and they had chased him away!

Mrs Gordon got her best room cleaned and resurrected successfully, fortunately no damage was done to her precious ornaments and she was still talking to me. I refrained from telling her to look on the bright side because at least she wouldn't need to pay to get her chimney swept that year!

As far as I was concerned, in the future, rearing baby squirrels was most definitely banned!

Some of the satisfaction of being a vet or vet nurse is being able to save animals lives, hand rearing baby animals or nursing sick, wild animals back to health and then releasing them back into their natural habitats. Many species are dealt with and some can present considerable challenges in both the handling and feeding of them. No matter how wild or unsociable an animal may be, it will always be given the same level of care and attention. Unfortunately for some, UK laws (Wildlife and Countryside Act 1981) now dictate that certain 'non-indigenous' species cannot be released into the wild after treatment even though they are already present and living in the wild before arriving for veterinary treatment! This is now the situation with Grey Squirrels although other non-native species such as game birds are legally released into the natural habitat in their thousands every year! The anomalies of life!

Tiny

How often in life are nicknames given to individuals which can mean exactly the opposite? This was exactly the case with Tiny.

One might imagine a pet named Tiny to be a small dog like a miniature Yorkshire Terrier or Chihuahua, perhaps even a small mouse or a hamster.

"Here's your next patient. It's Mrs Harris with Tiny," I was informed by the receptionist.

"Where are they?" I asked.

"Oh, they're just out at the car trying to get him in," was the answer. Hmm, how difficult could it be to encourage a pet called Tiny to enter a vet's surgery? I was soon to find out as the side door to the practice was pushed open and Mrs Harris and her barely teenage son, struggled to haul a sports bag over the doorstep. It was a rather large sports bag which they couldn't lift between them but which they were proceeding to drag into the building.

"Would you like a hand?" I asked. "Oh. Yes please," they both answered. As I endeavoured to lift the sports bag, which was really quite heavy, I said, "What in all the world have you got in here?"

"This is Tiny." replied Mrs Harris as her son made a quick exit through the door and went back to the car.

"And who in all the world is Tiny?" I asked her.

With some difficulty, I lifted the bag up and placed it on the consulting room table and then she replied. "Tiny is my 14-foot-long Python."

OK, I thought, and although a fourteen feet long python isn't an everyday patient, I will soon deal with him and get him fixed.

"So, what brings you here with Tiny?" I asked.

"He hasn't been eating," she replied. "In fact, he hasn't eaten for 5 months and I am getting very concerned about him."

"Let me have a look at him then," I said as I began to unzip the top of the sports bag.

"What are you doing?" she asked.

"I am going to examine him," I replied.

"Oh dear!" was the reply. "He is not going to like that!"

I proceeded to try and find his head, which is where one normally starts to examine an animal from, and found it underneath various coils of his body. He was, indeed, massive and he wasn't taking kindly to being interfered with! As I tried to extricate Tiny's front end from the bag he began hissing and wriggling in a rather irritable manner.

"I told you that he wouldn't like being examined." Mrs Harris stated what was becoming increasingly more obvious!

As part of the initial examination, I needed to have a look in his mouth to make sure that there were no signs of any issues such as infection or other oral problems and whilst holding Tiny by the neck, just behind his head, I turned around to reach for my snake mouth-gag, an instrument to aid opening his mouth without getting fingers caught on dozens of extremely sharp teeth and also without damaging the snake's mouth.

When Mrs Harris saw what I was about to open his mouth she exclaimed, "Oh dear! He's definitely not going to like this!"

She was absolutely correct of course and as I wrestled with Tiny, he started to stiffen his neck and upper body so that as I tried to open his mouth he rose vertically out of the sports bag and started hissing even more loudly as he faced me, his head now being higher up in the air than mine! Don't forget that 'Tiny' was 14-feet-long and only about 5-feet of his body length was out of the bag. I couldn't see any problems inside his mouth, and I then tried to put this rather stiff snake back into the bag! This was accomplished with some difficulty since the now angry Tiny didn't particularly want to go back into the bag! Eventually, I got his body back inside, started to zip the sports bag shut, whilst releasing Tiny's head at the very last moment! I didn't intend getting bitten by him! However, I also knew that I was going to need to get Tiny back out of the bag at some point for a more thorough examination of the rest of his body.

I turned towards Mrs Harris to discuss Tiny and about what I was going to do next.

Mrs Harris was a rather attractive, physically well endowed, lady who I had seen previously with other animals and on each occasion, she was, what a student approvingly described as being exotically dressed. Maybe he meant almost undressed, for even in cold weather she would appear in a mini skirt, bare legs and a skimpy top! On one occasion he was so engrossed with admiring her that he never even noticed that she had an animal with her!

Today was no exception, and an extremely short mini skirt was, yet again, part of her attire. As I faced towards her and with my back to the sports bag on the table, I felt a sudden thump on my back and as I half turned towards the bag, I saw Tiny who was by this time a third of the way out of the rapidly unzipping bag! I realised that the angry Tiny had struck at my back with his enormous mouth and many sharp teeth. Fortunately, I had enough clothing on so that I didn't feel the effect of the teeth, just that of the strike.

By this time, Tiny was rapidly exiting the bag and leaving the table in the opposite direction to which we were standing. He was obviously intent upon making a rapid escape! I moved quickly to try and grab him and stop him escaping but just as I did so Mrs Harris said, "I'll get him." By this time, Tiny had almost completely exited the sports bag, just his tail being in the bag and his head some 14-feet away. As Mrs Harris made a move to get hold of him, I saw his head turn back towards us and his mouth opened wide. In fact, really wide! I don't think that either of us actually saw what happened next, for, in an instant and as quick as a flash, Tiny doubled back on himself and flew through the air, hitting Mrs Harris on the upper part of her bare leg just under her rather miniscule skirt!

Fortunately, he didn't hang on but immediately let go and slithered off looking for a means of escape.

As he hit her leg with his mouth open she screamed and either jumped or was knocked backwards and in the process knocked me over too! Mrs Harris fell onto the sharps disposal bin and I ended up in the waste bin, both of us with our legs in the air, but with the view of Mrs Harris' spread-eagled legs being somewhat considerably more interesting than that of mine! Of course, I didn't stare! Well not too much! However, a pair of bare legs, snakeskin coloured panties and multiple teeth marks at the top of those legs will be etched on my mind forever!

Pythons have literally dozens of sharp teeth in both the upper and lower jaws and have the ability to open their mouths incredibly wide so that Tiny's gape could almost encompass Mrs Harris' whole upper thigh. She looked a bit shocked as I helped her to her feet and then as we both looked down she slightly raised the hem of her skirt. We then saw that her leg had a considerable amount of blood beginning to trickle down it from multiple teeth punctures! I quickly got some surgical gauze swabs and helped her to stem the flow of blood by applying pressure to the wounds. Fortunately, she was made of strong stuff and she didn't faint or pass out. Ensuring that she was OK and leaving her applying pressure to her wounds herself, I then went to find Tiny who, by this time, had escaped from the room and disappeared.

Hearing a commotion from the operating theatre which was at the end of an adjacent corridor, I surmised, because of the screams of panic, that Tiny might just have ended up there and indeed, he had! I rushed down the corridor to catch Tiny, only to find him slithering under the operating table and disappearing into the depths of the theatre. There were two colleagues in the operating theatre that morning, a vet and a vet nurse, who were engrossed in spaying a cat when they heard the shrieks and commotion emanating from the consulting area. They knew that there was an unusual patient in, because although there were human shrieks and the noise of bins falling over etc., there were no animal sounds. No barks, no meowing, no scrabbling of paws. The vet, in particular just happened to have a total phobia of snakes, particularly of large ones and she suddenly saw the door being pushed open and all 14-feet of Tiny began entering the room!

When I reached the operating theatre, I was confronted by the sight of an ashen-faced vet and similarly coloured vet nurse who were both on top of the operating table, still operating on the cat, whilst the escaped python was continuing his journey beneath the table! A mixture of total fear, but incredible dedication too!

I retrieved Tiny and then carried him back to Mrs Harris, not without some difficulty, for he was both quite heavy and not entirely pleased about being captured. By this time, her leg was bleeding less and she had regained her composure somewhat, but she certainly didn't offer to help as I manoeuvred the snake back into the sports bag, ensuring that this time it was tightly and completely zipped shut!

We never did find anything physically wrong with Tiny, apart from the fact that he was too well fed, extremely fat and grossly overweight. It was another whole year before he started eating properly again.

All is well that ends well! Mrs Harris had no lasting effects from her snake bites, the vet and vet nurse were none the worse for their little bit of excitement, the cat was successfully neutered, Tiny eventually started eating again and I didn't suffer any long-term psychological harm from my unexpected view of bare legs, short skirts and underwear!

The tail end of this tale was when I regaled one of my colleagues with the events that had happened.

He asked me, "Where, exactly did you say that she got bitten? It was the top of her thigh wasn't it? Did she have nice legs? Were the wounds right at the very top? Was there a lot of blood too? Did you have to attend to her wounds?"

I replied in the affirmative to all of the above and then he said, "And I bet, that although you know pythons are non-venomous, you felt obliged to get down and suck out all the poison!"

I was too slow and too innocent to think of that one! Maybe next time!

Early Morning Call Out

It was 1:00 a.m. on a wet November night and I had not been in bed very long, having been working non-stop all weekend, when the telephone started ringing. I must admit that I struggled to wake up having just fallen into a deep sleep from exhaustion.

As I picked up the receiver, a rather agitated voice could be heard shouting down the phone.

"You've got to get over here straight away and put my dog to sleep."

It was not uncommon to get inebriated people phoning up either late on a Saturday night or early Sunday morning when they were feeling either brave or irrational. Sadly, some of these calls were hoaxes or, on occasion, abusive, e.g. "Is that the vet? Well, you just get your f…g backside over here, I've a hamster that need seeing." Patience, tact, and diplomacy are often needed and of course at the end of the day we are obliged to see any animal that is in distress, no matter how obnoxious the owner may be. All these qualities can often be in short supply when one is physically and emotionally shattered and suffering from huge sleep deprivation!

"Put to sleep? At this time of night? Has it been injured or is it really unwell?" There are few 'put to sleep' emergencies in the middle of the night, although some people will mysteriously decide that, this is now the exact time that this deed needs to be carried out! Usually because they have been fortified by prodigious amounts of alcoholic beverage!

The voice at the other end of the phone was sounding increasingly more agitated as he repeated, "You must come quickly, it's really urgent. He has tried to attack us and he's gone and eaten our other dog…and I fear that we are going to be next! I have been onto the police and they said that we had to phone you! Please, please come quickly."

The man certainly sounded agitated, and he didn't sound like the usual drunk, so I tried to ascertain the exact circumstances from him and whereabouts he lived. He told me which town he lived in, which was about 10 miles away and as I attempted to get his address, I heard him say, "My phone's dying, there's not much battery power left," then a click and silence as his phone actually did die!

By now I was wide awake, but still a bit irritated about being disturbed at 1 a.m.! Dogs just don't suddenly become aggressive at that time of the morning or maybe it really was a hoax?

The problem, now, of course was that I didn't have the guy's address and I really hoped that if it was a genuine call that he would phone back. Ten minutes or so later, he still hadn't phoned back and so the only course of action that I could think of was to telephone the local police station that covered the area where they lived.

"Fairfield police, Can I help you?"

I explained who I was and how I had received this strange call about a dog attacking its owner and how I didn't get the person's address before his phone died. I told the police call handler that he was supposed to have phoned them a short while earlier and I was concerned that maybe it was a hoax call.

"Oh no, it definitely isn't a hoax." she said, "This man phoned about half an hour ago, but we were far too busy to attend, being the usual, manic Saturday night dealing with people who have partaken of too much 'refreshment'! I told him to phone you."

Oh well, that explained the phone call. "Do you happen to know the address because his phone died mid-call?"

Fortunately, she gave me a note of the address and so I tumbled out of bed, got dressed and drove the ten miles to the house, musing that it wasn't in a particularly salubrious part of the town! How wonderful to be out and about in the middle of a cold, wet November night!

Eventually, I arrived at the house in question. It was a three-storey terraced house which was completely dark. There wasn't a light on anywhere! *Strange*, I thought to myself as I opened the front gate and took three strides along the garden path to the front door. I found the bell and rang it. No response from within the house! I rang it again, and then again and again. There was still no response and so I hammered on the door with my fist, determined to get the occupants to answer the door. There was complete silence and there was no sign at all of anybody being in the house.

Maybe it was a hoax after all. I returned to my car and telephoned the police station once more.

"There is nobody at the address that you gave me!" I said to the call handler. "Perhaps it really was a hoax?"

"I don't think it was a hoax," she replied, "He sounded really stressed out and frightened but he did give me his father-in-law's address. Maybe they have gone there."

I duly noted down the new address and set off to find it. Fortunately, it was only about three streets away and turned out to be a pensioner's bungalow which was also in total darkness! Once again, I rang the bell numerous times and knocked loudly on the front door. At this stage, I was determined to get somebody up out of their bed because I hadn't come all this was way in the middle of the night without getting some sort of result. Eventually, I heard some stirring within the depths of the house and a light was switched on in the hallway. The door opened a small way and a very gruff, annoyed sounding voice shouted.

"Who is it and what do you want?"

I explained who I was and how I had been given this address by the police. I had obviously just wakened up a very sleepy old man, wearing pyjamas and who was busily tying his dressing gown cord.

"I have been given your address by the police. I'm the vet who was called out to see a German Shepherd that had attacked somebody. Is the dog yours?"

"No! It most certainly isn't mine and it isn't here," he grumbled.

"Well, where is it then?" I asked with a certain degree of irritation because I was getting wet, and I was cold and tired. It was, after all, the middle of the night and I should have been sleeping in a nice warm bed.

"It's up the road at my son in law's house. Here are the keys for you to go in and put it to sleep."

"The keys? What? Do you mean for the house that I have just been at?"

"Yes, that is the house," and he tried to give me the keys again.

"Why is your son-in-law not in the house, and just where is he?" I asked him.

"He's gone to Grangetown for safety."

"Grangetown! For safety?" I questioned him. "Why in all the world has he gone there when he has just called me out?"

"He's gone there for safety," was the response.

"Safety?" I asked him as I became even more irritated.

"Oh yes! For safety. You see, the dog knows his way down here and he was terrified that he would track them down to here and then attack them. My son-in-law is a big man, and he doesn't scare easily but he was absolutely terrified. I have never seen anybody who was as scared as that! He would normally face up to anything, but he was shaking like a leaf." And he repeated the fact that his son-in-law was a 'big man who doesn't scare easily'. "Here, you take the keys and go and put him to sleep."

I stood and argued with him and told him that there was no way that I was going into somebody's house, myself, in the middle of the night. "You, come with me and I will go in but I'm not going in alone." I could be accused of stealing or damaging anything whilst I was in the house, especially realising the area that I was in.

"Me, come with you? Ha! You must be joking! There is absolutely no way that I'm going anywhere near that dog! If it scares my son-in-law rigid, then I am just definitely not going!" He then added, "I will tell you how bad it was. My son-in-law arrived at my house in a compete panic and he was hammering on the door. We were in our beds and thought he was going to knock the door down! I will tell you how really bad it was because he was standing there trembling and shaking like a leaf," and then added, "And he had no clothes on! Not a stitch! And my daughter was no better! She jumped out the car and ran up to the house and she hadn't any clothes on either! Nothing!"

He then explained how they had to provide them with clothes so that they could drive to their other in-laws in Grangetown for safety. "They were both shaking so badly that they could hardly get their borrowed clothes on!"

I was trying to imagine the scene and although getting a bit annoyed at the night's events, I couldn't stop wishing that I had arrived a lot sooner so I could have seen the sights! Apparently, the couple had tumbled out of bed and just ran down their stairs as fast as they could, only stopping to grab the car keys and then driving, totally naked, through the streets to safety!

"Right, get some clothes on," I said to the old man, "and come with me up to the house."

"Absolutely, no way! If that dog was going to attack my son-in-law, who doesn't scare easily, and he's a big strong man, then I am certainly not going anywhere near him! He's a great big dog you know!"

"Well, I am not going home until we get this sorted out. I haven't got out of bed for nothing! Can you not get in touch with your son-in-law?"

Just as this altercation was reaching a stalemate, a car screeched to a halt outside the house. The doors opened and a young couple dashed up the short drive to where I was standing. They were rather oddly dressed, particularly on the part of the man, whose trousers were at half-mast and who was also wearing an ill-fitting jacket! His wife was enveloped in a large jumper and a long flowing skirt, the waistband of which she had to hang on to, to stop it falling down.

"Are you the vet?" the man asked me in a rather shaky voice, which was not surprising since he was either very cold or very frightened of something! "Have you been up and put him to sleep?" he said in a strangulated, tremulous voice.

"Of course not!" I retorted, "Because you weren't here, and this man wouldn't go up to the house with me. Anyway, where in all the world have you been?"

"We were at my parents in Grangetown. We went there for safety because that dog has gone absolutely crazy. He's killed our Jack Russell and I knew that we were next because of the way that he was looking at us. He h-h-ha-ad t-t-that l-l-look i-in-n h-h-his e-e-eyes and I j-j-just knew that we were going to be next as he l-l-looked at us." I thought he was going to burst into tears as his words became more stilted and his whole being started shaking even more!

"So why did you arrive back?" I asked him.

"Well, I phoned your wife when we got to Grangetown in order to check that you were actually coming. She gave me a row and asked me what I was doing in Grangetown and to get straight back up the road to our house in Fairfield because you would be already there."

"I will give you the keys," he said, "and you can go up and 'see to' the dog."

"I have just been through all of this with your father-in-law, and I am definitely not going into your house without somebody being there! Absolutely not! You have to come with me."

"I can't do that. Please, please don't make me! He will 'have me' if he sees me! He's a big strong dog and he's already killed our other dog you know."

At this point, I thought that he was in danger of passing out! He was a tall man and he had a long way to fall! We eventually, after a lot of persuasion, agreed that he would come up to the house with me but he that wouldn't get out of the car! He would sit in the car with the engine running and the car door open and I would go into the house. His reasoning was that if the dog managed to get past me then he was ready to shut his door and drive rapidly off!

Thus, we arrived at the house and with shaking hands he handed me the keys to the house which was dark. I unlocked the door and carefully opened it. There was no sound or sign of life and so I reached for the light switch and found that I was in an empty kitchen. So far, so good! At the far end of the kitchen was a closed door and I made my way over to it and slowly opened it. I couldn't see a thing in the darkness and I had to shout back to the man in his car to ask him where the light switches were. His trembling reply informed me that the light switch to the stairs was on the left-hand side. Just as I went to switch the lights on, I had a sudden thought. What was I going to say to this huge German shepherd, of uncertain temperament and of murderous intent, if I met him coming down the stairs?

"What is his name?" I yelled. Now, if there was ever a name that I didn't want to hear, it was the one that I heard.

"He's called…W-W-Wol-lf."

"Wolf!" I confirmed. Fantastic! Just what I needed to hear!

This was, of course, a three-storied house and so there were a lot of rooms to check and quite a few flights of stairs to ascend, not knowing at which point I was going to encounter the killer called Wolf!

I slowly and warily advanced up the stairs and carefully checked each room and reached the very top of the house, leaving one remaining room to check! The strangest thing was that I hadn't heard a sound from anywhere apart from the owner who was busy keeping his car engine revved up, just in case! I thought that I might have heard a growl or a bark as I was, quite obviously, an intruder coming into the house in the middle of the night! Maybe Wolf was possessed of great cunning and was just waiting his chance to launch himself at me and to finish me off? The silent killer!

In my experience, aggressive German Shepherds always launched themselves at one's throat, and all that I had for defence was a rope dog lead and my medical case! I had a few near misses in the past treating security dogs, garage guard dogs and Ministry of Defence 'stop' dogs. At least some of them, but not all of them, had muzzles on! I reassured myself that all you needed was confidence and dominance in dealing with rogue dogs and I had plenty of experience. However, none of them were called Wolf!

I saw a chink of light shining from under the door of the last room to be searched. I took a deep breath as I thought that the dreadful 'Wolf' must be in there and started to open the door, very slowly, but being ready to shut it quickly again if needed! There was absolute silence and then I heard panting! He was definitely in there! I squinted through the crack that I had opened, keeping a good hold of the door handle in case it needed to be shut quickly and I peered inside.

What a scene of chaos! The bed had been overturned, the wardrobe had fallen over and there was a complete disarray of bed, clothes and even the bedside cabinet on top of the bed! Still no growling or barking, just the sound of fast and loud panting! Wolf must be lurking behind the door!

I had no other option but to push the door open a little bit more, all the time being ready for the attack on my throat! However, as I looked down at the carpet, with the door now slightly ajar, I saw four fore legs! Canine front legs; two smaller ones and on either side of them two very large hairy legs! Doh! Was 'Wolf' some sort of werewolf with eight legs?

I pushed the door open a little bit more and there standing between the legs of this enormous, hairy German Shepherd dog was a little Jack Russell, happily wagging its tail! It seemed to me to be very much alive and far too active to have been the subject of a canine murder! Ignoring the Jack Russell, I turned my attention to Wolf, who was panting really hard by this time, probably due to the intense heat in the room. In my firmest and most dominant, yet kind voice, I said, "Right 'Wolf', let's be having you," and I confidently slipped a running lead over his head. "That's a good boy. You're coming with me. Out you come. There's a good dog."

He obediently and without any problem came forward out of the room from which a considerable heat and 'doggy poo' smell was emanating! The room was completely and utterly trashed, and even the dressing table had been upended!

Oh well I thought to myself as I carefully proceeded down the stairs with 'Wolf', leaving the Jack Russell behind. I mused, "Strangely, considering the circumstances, he seems oddly compliant and is offering no resistance at all, considering that he doesn't even know me."

"I've got him!" I shouted as I entered the kitchen.

"Oh no! Please, please don't let him see me! He will attack me!" said the owner as he shut the car door and shouted out the window. "Just take him away, please!" and he wound up his window.

"Right Wolf, jump in the car," I ordered and he obediently leapt into the cage in the back of my car.

Phew, that wasn't too bad in the end, I thought and went back to the owner who was still gripping the steering wheel of the car, whilst sweating and shaking.

"Right, switch off the engine and come into the house," I said to him.

"Aaaaare you sure he's safely locked away?" he stammered.

"Yes, he's locked up in the back of my car. Let us go into the house and you can tell me what happened, and we can also settle up for the night call."

He reluctantly left the safety of the car and we both made our way into the kitchen. Wolf's owner was indeed a big man, in fact a big, trembling, shivering man who was still barely coherent!

He began to describe what had taken place and as he spoke, I could see the absolute terror in his face as he recounted the night's events.

"We were both asleep in our bed when we were woken up by this terrible commotion beyond the foot of our bed. It was completely dark, of course, and when I switched on the bedside light, I could see W-W-Wolf and then I noticed that our Jack Russell was gone! He'd obviously killed him and now he was looking at us and I just knew that we were going to be next!" He shuddered as he remembered how Wolf had this terrible look in his eyes. "He just was looking at me with this terrible expression. He was looking right through me with this really weird, glazed expression. He was salivating too, and I just knew that he was going to attack me. I realised what he had done to our other dog and so, without any hesitation and as quickly as I could I grabbed my wife, hauled her out of bed and tipped the bed and the wardrobe over to stop him following us!" He shuddered as he spoke. "It was just awful, I really don't know how we got out in time!" He continued to tremble as he stammered and stuttered over his words.

"We ran out into the car and drove off as quickly as we could to my in-laws and then realised that we had no clothes on! We had to borrow some from them! I phoned the police, but they were too busy to attend and then they told me just to phone you. I then realised that Wolf knew his way down to my in-laws and that he would track us down and attack us there, so we had to go off to Grangetown for safety." He was still shaking and was becoming visibly more and more upset as he re-lived the night's happenings and his brush with death!

"Calm down, you are fine, and no dogs are going to attack you tonight," I said.

"But he still m-m-might if he gets out your c-c-car," he responded. "He's a big, powerful dog and he's already killed our other dog tonight. I am certain that we would have been his next victims!"

I then had to gently explain to him how his other dog was still alive and up in his bedroom and that the last time that I saw him he was unscathed and was wagging his little tail!

"W-W-What?" was all he could manage to stutter. "How could that be because he's dead?"

I then had to try and piece together the events of the night and make some sense of it all. What had actually happened was that the two dogs were both sleeping peacefully on the floor at the foot of the bed when Wolf presumably took an epileptic fit; (not uncommon in some German Shepherds).

The Jack Russell got a fright at the sudden commotion of Wolf's convulsions and dived under some furniture out of harm's way. Wolf obviously was having a full-blown fit, with flailing legs, champing jaws, chattering of his pretty impressive teeth, salivating and evacuating his bladder and bowels on the bedroom carpet. His owners just woke up as he was coming out of the fit and when they switched the light on, they saw the glazed disorientated look in his eyes as 'he looked right through them'! The irony being that in his post-fit state he probably wasn't seeing them at all!

My explanation didn't do anything at all to reassure the owner and even though it was possible to treat the suspected epilepsy he never wanted to set eyes on Wolf again! I suspect that he had always been a bit scared of Wolf who his father-in-law had described as being of uncertain temperament!

"Please just take him away! That's all I want. We couldn't go through all that again. I feel so lucky to be alive! Let me pay you now."

Well, that was another saga because he had no money, and his hands were still shaking so much that he could neither hold his chequebook nor write the cheque! I had to write the cheque out for him and then just ask him to sign it. That in itself was another problem because when he tried to write, his hand was going up and down across the page like the stylus on a lie detector!

As I left the house, I wondered whether the bank would ever accept his signature on the cheque, and I thought about the events of the night. I called to mind the immortal words of the great Siegfried Farnon. "James, you must always attend, attend, attend!" I just regretted that I hadn't attended a little bit more swiftly in which case I might have seen the nude exodus from the house too!

It's a Hard Life!

There can be little doubt that the life of a large animal, or farm vet, is definitely both mentally and physically arduous. When one is young and fit, a bit more athletic than when one is older, bashes and bruises and lack of sleep just don't seem to be a problem. Life and the wear and tear on one's body eventually begins to take its toll and by about 55 years of age, night calls lose their excitement and bodily injuries take so much longer to heal!

Although there is a huge amount of satisfaction in delivering a live calf, attending a cow calving can be both extremely physically tiring and also can take up a large amount of 'sleeping time' if one has to perform a caesarean in the middle of the night. Years ago, before large continental breeds became popular, caesareans were relatively uncommon operations. Most calvings were just a question of sorting out calves that were attempting to be brought into this world in the wrong position or were maybe twins that were tangled up in the womb. However, nowadays with larger calves there are many more operations performed to ensure a successful, live delivery.

The phone would ring in the early hours of the morning and more often than not it would always be 'the boss' telling you to go an attend to a calving!

"Are you in your bed?" was his cheery greeting. "Most people die in their beds you know! There's a cow needing help at Macpherson's, Drygate, you had better go and see what needs done." The greeting was cheery because he wasn't going to have to get out of his own bed! We had a fairly common system in a large animal practice covering a huge area of having a 'first' on call with another person being the 'second' on call in case there were too many calls for the on-duty vet to cope with or in case they needed some sort of assistance. It worked out fairly well in a multi-man practice but when there were only three in the practice, and where the 'boss' had an unusual sense of logic, then it meant having to work almost every night of the week and two weekends on call out of three.

If I was first on call, I would quite naturally expect to do all the night work. However, the next night I would be second on call and more often than not I would still get the call outs! How could that happen?

Ring, ring, ring; the phone was demanding my attention. "Hello, there's a difficult calving at Abermore. Now I know I'm first on call, but it is 30 miles away and therefore you had better go to it, seeing you are second on call. I'm first on call and so I had better hang about here in case something happens!" The twisted logic never failed him, but there was no choice but to get out of bed and go! Another night with three hours of sleep lost, and tomorrow another busy day!

The only time that the system failed him was on one Hogmanay. I was first on call and hoping for a quiet night.

Travelling about was going to be difficult anyway if I had to venture out because the whole area was covered in deep snow. Hopefully, few people would be needing our help that night.

I stayed up late in order that I might 'see in' the New Year with my flatmate and then went off to bed, hoping to get a good sleep.

It couldn't have been more than an hour that I had been asleep when the phone rang. I was instantly awake and crawled out of bed to answer it. A very anxious sounding lady was on the other end of the line. It was Mrs Robb, the boss's wife.

"I am so worried about my husband. He went away to a cow calving about four hours ago and hasn't returned yet. I have phoned the farm and I can't get an answer. Do you think that you could go and see if he needs any help and maybe check that his car hasn't got stuck in the snow? I know that it's a rotten night with all this snow but the farm, Dunlavity, is away in the hills and anything could have happened to him."

"Yes, of course," I replied, "That's not a problem," but at the same time thinking how odd it was that the boss had actually gone out on a call to a far-away farm on an atrocious night of weather and especially when I was first on call! Unheard of! Maybe he was full of festive good will?

The snow was deep and the wind was causing it to drift across the road so that any previous car tyre tracks were obliterated! There were no car tracks to follow and I had to drive exceedingly carefully. The weather was deteriorating and I could hardly see more than a few feet in front of the car. It was an extremely slow journey now that I had left the main road and I began to wonder if the boss had ended up coming off the road! Dunlavity just had to be another 10 miles away near the end of a remote glen!

Eventually, I arrived at the farm and found it to be completely dark! Maybe everyone was in the byre round the back. A quick reconnoitre didn't reveal anything nor any recent signs of a calving having taken place. I made my way through the snow to the farmhouse door and knocked on it. There was no response. I hammered on the door as loudly as I could and eventually, I heard footsteps coming through the kitchen. Mr Montgomery had the reputation of being pretty grumpy and tonight he certainly lived up to that reputation. They didn't get many visitors and especially not in the middle of the night! It wouldn't have surprised me if he had appeared with his shotgun!

"What do YOU want?" he grunted.

"Mr Robb was here to see a cow calving and he hasn't returned. Mrs Robb, asked me to come and see if he needed a hand. She couldn't get through on the phone."

"Phone line is down with the snow and he hasn't been here. No cows calving 'til spring. Good night!" and with that he slammed the door shut!

This of course was in the days before mobile phones had been invented and I had no option but to carefully retrace my steps and keep an eye out for Mr Robb's car. On the other hand he hadn't been at Dunlavity, perhaps his wife had got the wrong farm name? The journey home was slightly easier since the wind had dropped and I could see some of my own car tracks. Eventually, I arrived home and phoned up Mrs Robb.

"Is everything alright? Did you find him?" she almost shouted down the phone. "I'm at my wits end with worry."

"He wasn't there," I replied. "Are you sure that you got the correct farm?" I asked.

"Absolutely certain! I am sorry to have got you out on such a bad night," her voice faded off into sobbing and she put the receiver down.

It was an unusual start to New Year's morning. The phone rang mid-morning for the very first time that year. It was Mr Robb, absolutely incandescent with rage! He bellowed down the phone, "What do you think you were doing last night? Don't you ever, ever do that again!"

"What do you mean?" I asked.

"You will never, ever go out looking for me again no matter what my wife says! Never! Do you hear?"

I was somewhat taken aback by his explosion. *Happy New Year!* I thought! I hadn't done anything wrong, or had I?

I puzzled over it all, then it dawned on me! The boss would never have gone to a cow calving when I was first on call and it was Hogmanay. He had spun his wife a yarn, choosing a fictitious visit to a far-flung farm as a cover for him going to another Hogmanay event! 'Be sure that your sins will find you out' was my old Grannies maxim! Proven correct again!

The end result of the 'calving that never was', was the successful delivery of a divorce for the boss! Working relationships were never the same again after that, especially when the affair was found to be with a staff member. Somehow, it seemed to be all my fault!

I moved away to another practice shortly afterwards.

Snow was commonly experienced in Highland winters and people just accepted it as part of everyday weather but occasionally there would be an incredibly severe snowfall that would temporarily bring normal travel and work activities to a halt. In one such winter, the practice was cut off from the outside world by snowdrifts that were up to 20-feet-deep in places! Life was certainly disrupted because there were few places that we could reach by car until the roads were cleared. Our practice covered a vast area of the Highlands and the neighbouring practice to the North was quite a long distance away, beyond a range of hills. They too, would be snowed in and restricted to doing visits in the less affected coastal areas.

"I wonder if you would be good enough to help us out?" said the voice on the phone. "We have been asked to attend a cow calving at Glen Blair and we can't get there from this end because of the snow. We would need to walk about nine miles up the glen through deep snow to get there. Do you think that you could get a bit nearer from your end and go through the pass from Glen Branter…it would only entail about a one mile walk for you?"

My boss took the phone from the receptionist. "Of course, we will do our best. I will send one of the young fit lads. They're sitting here doing nothing and need the exercise! A walk will do them good! Ha, ha!"

I was 'volunteered' to go, seeing that I was the most junior member of staff. "You will need to go up Glen Branter for as far as you can and then you will need to leave your car and walk through the gap in the hills to Glen Blair. The farmer will meet you…if he can get up the track! Oh, and it's a heifer that's been trying to calve for a while apparently!"

That was just the news that I didn't want to hear. A heifer having difficulty could present significant problems. *Oh well!* I thought, *I'll see when I get there*. The driving was slow and hazardous and it took much longer than it would have done normally to get up the glen. It had not snowed now for twenty-four hours but the last night's severe frost had not only caused ice to form on the roads but had also frozen the snow drifts so that walking was quite difficult. Added to that was a sharp, biting wind in what was otherwise a sunny, clear day.

I eventually had to abandon my car and start walking! What would I need to take with me? I had equipped myself with a 5-litre backpack of warm water before I had left the practice and gathering up obstetrical lubricant, disinfectant, calving ropes, my calving gown and with some injections in my pockets I set off through the pass towards Glen Blair. I was hoping that I had remembered to take everything that I might need.

Surprisingly, the walking wasn't as bad as I had anticipated because the snow was pretty hard and frozen and I was walking on the top of the drifts. I thought that it must be like walking to the North Pole! The farmer who was supposedly coming to meet me never appeared because his vehicles were snowed in and I eventually reached his steading.

"Thanks for coming lad, but I don't know what you're going to do because she has been calving since yesterday morning, possibly even during the previous night, but there was no chance of anybody getting here until today. Have you got what you need? She is about half a mile away, and she's down and can't get up."

It was getting worse and worse! I had naively expected that she might be in a byre or even next to the steading but another walk? "Have you got a bucket?" I asked, "I've got water in this pack on my back."

"Right, off we go then. Have you been qualified for very long?"

Just great, I thought, not only are all the conditions adverse ones but he's now questioning my experience. He strode off in the opposite direction to the one in which I had come by and I trudged after him with a degree of despondency. The snow was so deep and hard that we were actually walking over the top of five-barred field gates without actually seeing them! It was so cold too!

"Not far now," he shouted above the wind. "There she is over there by that big drift. She can't get up. Been down now for over a day. Should have called you yesterday but you wouldn't have got here."

My heart sank even further. Here was a cow lying in the snow, unable to get up and exhausted from the exertion of trying to produce a calf and what's more, I was going to have to lie down in the snow behind her and try and fix the problem, whatever it was! I reluctantly peeled off my coat and jacket and quickly donned my calving gown. It was absolutely freezing, standing there in sub-zero temperatures with my arms, bare to my arm pits and exposed to the elements. I hurriedly poured some disinfectant and the, by now, cold water into the bucket and lay down in the snow behind the heifer so that I could examine her. I would need to be quick resolving this problem otherwise I was going to freeze to death!

As I explored her swollen passage with a well-lubricated arm, I encountered a relatively small front leg. This was an encouraging discovery because it meant that the calf was small, possibly she was having twins, or maybe just a small calf lying in the wrong position to be born. I could fix either of those issues and soon get my clothes back on again. There was virtually no possibility of the calf being alive, unfortunately, and this fact was never conducive to ending with a happy or a satisfactory outcome.

As I explored the depth of the cow's vaginal passage it became apparent that there was only one calf present and with dismay, I discovered why the calf hadn't been born naturally. The joints of its limbs were totally immobile and ankylosed so that it could not be manipulated into anything like a normal delivery position! How was I going to get it out? There was no possibility of performing a caesarean in these conditions without totally risking the cow's life and in any case, I didn't have a surgical kit with me!

In many ways, it was fortunate that the calf had died since that afforded opportunities to deal with it without resorting to surgery. One of those would have been to 'dismantle' the calf, a process called embryotomy, using a special 'cheese wire' to cut the limbs and head off. For the vet, it is an energy sapping, strenuous process sawing through bones with the wire but fortunately, for the cow it is painless. My problem with this calving was that my 'wire' was still in my car a few snow-covered miles away!

Absolute desperation and determination can sometime give you extra strength and this is what happened here. The farmer had wandered off when he realised that there would be no living calf and when he didn't fancy freezing to death while I wrestled with the dead calf! My only solution to the ankylosed joints problem was to make a superhuman effort and break the joints with my bare hands or to be more accurate with one hand! Attaching ropes to the legs and with plenty of lubrication I was then able, sometime later, to deliver the deformed calf.

Job done! After hurriedly washing my arms and my calving gown down with the remains of the disinfectant I hurriedly got back into my jacket and waterproofs. Strangely enough, I was no longer cold and was, in fact sweating profusely! The cow got the benefit of some injections. I left her and went to find the farmer and to give him advice and instructions on further care for his animal. I strongly suspect that he had left me because he was looking and feeling decidedly queasy once he heard the bones breaking!

It was still quite a strenuous walk back to my car through the snow, but I returned to it with a much happier heart! I just had to hope that my vehicle wasn't snow bound!

It is the most satisfying and exhilarating experience to attend a difficult calving and deliver a live calf but on the other hand it can be really quite depressing and disheartening delivering a dead calf because although one is saving the mother's life one can feel the disappointment and sadness of the farmer who will suffer a financial loss with having no calf to rear that year.

One of the nicest episodes that sticks in my memory was being called out at about 11:30 p.m. on a warm, mid-June evening when, being in the North of Scotland, there was still some daylight. The visit was to a cow that belonged to a crofter that was having difficulty calving. Most crofters were fairly poor, financially, and the loss of a cow or calf could have a major impact upon their income. It could, in fact, be quite catastrophic! These particular people were extremely poor but were also as hospitable and kindly as anybody could be. I arrived at the croft and went into the byre to find a cow with the two front feet of a calf protruding from its vagina. She had been pushing for a couple of hours and hadn't made any progress, hence the request for help.

I examined the cow and realised that the calf's head wasn't engaging with the passage and so with relative ease the problem was sorted and a live calf delivered, both to mine and the crofter's delight and relief. The most amazing thing about that time of year was that as I headed home, the light was just starting to get brighter again and it had never actually become properly dark. It is an indescribable feeling to have successfully completed a live delivery for lovely people and to cap it all, to do it on an amazing summer's night. A joy to be out and about and alive!

Wintertime was a completely different scenario when days were short and the nights were long and it could also be extremely dark! Travelling about in the depths of remote countryside on a black, dark night with no moonlight was an almost surreal experience. Although some of the country folk lived in poor or impoverished conditions, I was totally dumbfounded to be called out to a remote croft one evening where there was no electricity, no telephone and no water supply either! I had never been to this particular place before and it really was truly remote! I had long since left the main road, travelled along a rutted lane before coming across a little wooden sign, 'Drumbeck Croft' which pointed across a field!

In my car headlights, I picked out a grassy track and so I followed it until I came to a small cottage with steading attached. It was in total darkness. Had I arrived at the wrong place?

I got out of my car and peered into the blackness of the night trying to see where the door to the house was. I heard a door open and shut but still couldn't see anything. I was so wishing that I had brought a torch and silently vowed that I would always carry one in the future!

"You the vet? Thank you for coming," spoken in a soft Highland accent. I almost jumped out of my skin as a figure spoke from behind me! "She's been trying to calve for a wee while now, a few hours I suppose, by the time I noticed her and walked to the phone box and back."

"What's happening with her?" I asked him as I gathered my calving ropes, disinfectant and lubrication together.

"I can only feel one leg and a head," was the reply, "and she's been pushing like mad. She doesn't usually have problems. She's quite an old lass now."

At least, she isn't a heifer I thought to myself, an older cow would be easier to work inside.

"OK. Have you got a bucket of warm water please?"

"Er no! Sorry, I don't have a bucket, but I'll get you a basin from the kitchen. No hot water either I'm afraid. The fire's gone out. You'll just need to use the water from the trough!"

This was certainly a new experience! A steading without a bucket and cold water out of a cattle trough! Could it get any worse? As it turned out, why yes it could!

Mr Fraser disappeared into the darkness, and I mean really disappeared, returning a few moments later with a chipped, shallow enamel basin. He dipped it into the water trough and then proceeded in the direction of what I assumed was the byre. I could hardly see him, but I could certainly hear the water sloshing back and forth and flowing over the top of the basin as he walked. The wind was getting up too and hit us fully in the face as we rounded the corner of the steading. He pushed the byre door open with his back and I entered a cosy, warm byre behind him.

"Could you switch the lights on?" I asked, as I heard him place the basin on the ground.

"Don't have any electricity up here!" was his reply.

"Well, how exactly am I going to see the cow?" I asked him.

"I'll fetch some matches," Mr Fraser said and disappeared out of the door leaving me in the byre where I had absolutely no visibility whatsoever! Maybe he had an oil lamp or similar. That would be good I thought.

Duncan appeared a short while later and produced a match which he struck against the matchbox, only to see it flare, splutter and get extinguished by the wind coming through the door!

"Damn!" he muttered. "I've only two matches left!" and with that, having closed the door he struck another one. The flickering match allowed me to see a few shorthorn cows lying in the standings in the byre. "That's her there," he said, pointing to the only cow that was standing and then that match too flickered and died.

"Don't you have a lamp?" I asked him. "I thought that was what the matches were for?"

"It got smashed and I've not got another one." And with that comment he struck the final match which stayed lit long enough for me to get behind the cow and place the basin on the floor behind it!

Now we were in absolute and total darkness! And I was reduced to aiming some disinfectant into where I thought the water in the basin was and then dropping my calving ropes in as well. This whole scene was becoming unreal as I had to feel my way up and down the cow's hind legs from the basin to her vaginal passage where I could feel one leg protruding from it. Fortunately, she was old and petted and I suspect tired from her exertions too, so there was very little resistance or objection from her. If she had been a 'kicker' then we would have definitely been in trouble!

Once I had my arm inside the cow, the lack of light made little difference to the proceedings because it was dark inside there anyway! I found the calf's head and also the reason for her obstetrical difficulties. One of the legs had bent backwards and so the calf had been unable to be born. With a lot of effort and some brute strength, I managed to repel the calf back into the womb, just enough so that I could get the offending leg back up into the normal position. Once it was sorted the old cow seemed to sense all was now well and she started to strain and push against me and the calf was then fairly easily delivered.

Was it alive or dead though? Between us, we managed to gently support the calf and laid it on the ground in the middle of the byre behind the cow. Just as I was beginning to think that it was dead, I heard a snort as it shook its head to clear its airways while flapping its ears against the side of its head. Fantastic! It was alive. Mother cow started calling to her baby and in complete darkness we pulled the calf up to her front end and heard her starting to lick it!

I followed the sound of Duncan's tackety boots and exited the byre into the inky black night, relieved that all had ended well. All that remained was to get washed up and by leaving my car door open I was able to shed a little bit of light on my ablutions which, by necessity, had to take place using water from the water trough that was fed by a spring. It was cold, extremely cold but somehow exhilarating too. Perhaps it was just a successful outcome to the night's work that made it feel like that. Whatever the reason, I certainly resolved that night to never be without a powerful torch or lantern in the future!

It is quite remarkable how many of the night time call outs ended up being adventures either in a stressful way or maybe, after reflection, a source of some amusement. The agricultural world has many characters and the part of the Highlands that I worked in seemed to have more than its particular fair share of them!

One such character was Willie Mackenzie who lived on a small croft with his sister. His holding had really steep fields in which he kept a few sheep and cows and on which he practised his own particular version of farming! Sadly, Willie was affected by a fairly severe form of epilepsy and was prone to taking frequent fits. In an attempt to control them, he took fairly hefty doses of medication, but despite these drugs he would, without any warning, still have the occasional seizure.

The result of taking so many anticonvulsant medicines was that he was pretty sleepy most of the day but became wide awake at night when the rest of us were attempting to sleep! He was a kindly, inoffensive old soul and always did his best to assist the vets when they were attending to animals on his croft. His sister provided prodigious amounts of scones and cups of tea and she also never failed to provide buckets of scalding hot water together with the obligatory soap and towel. One soon learned to check the temperature of the water before plunging one's hands into her 'hot water' because it was never far from boiling point!

As a recent employee of the practice, the one thing that I was warned about, apart from the scalding water, was never,

ever to accept a lift from Willie on his tractor. It wasn't just a question of careering down the steep field with him on an old rusty machine with suspect brakes, but it was also the risk that at any point he could take a fit whilst driving!

It was about 11:30 p.m. when my phone rang. It was my boss. "There's a heifer having difficulty calving at Willie Mackenzie's. He thinks the big Charolais bull from the next farm must have got at her so it's likely to be a caesarean. As usual he sounds as wide awake as anything and he never fails to phone up at night when his meds are wearing off! I will come with you because it will be quicker and more efficient that way because you know how he's pretty useless! As useful as a chocolate teapot!"

The croft wasn't too far away from the practice and we were soon there, being greeted by the happy, always whistling, Willie. He was much more awake than either of us felt.

"Hello boys how are you both tonight?" he greeted us, together with a toothless grin.

"She's in the byre here. I thinks she's trying to have a muckle big calf. It's yon great big white bull along the road, I think. Hope you can get it out OK."

We went into the byre and there was the aforementioned heifer standing before us with two extremely large calf's feet protruding from her vaginal passage. A quick examination confirmed that she would definitely need a caesarean since there was no way that the large calf could make its entry into the world via the normal route!

We were just about to start getting our equipment ready for the operation when the dim lights in the byre started flickering on and off and then the whole place went dark.

"Well, Willie, we certainly can't manage to do the op in the dark!" My boss drily observed.

"Never you fear! I will rig something up," replied Willie as he disappeared into his workshop. "This is always happening." We heard Willie happily whistling away to himself as he rummaged about in his workshop.

"Let's get this beast tied up outside. We can start doing the op under the car headlamps. I know Willie of old and he has no concept of time, speed nor electrical safety!"

We duly manhandled the heifer into the lean-to hay shed and tied her up and then moved the car so that its headlights illuminated the cow's flank. Working as rapidly as we could, we clipped the heifer's flank, anaesthetised her and started the op. It is so much more efficient having two vets working together than doing it alone, especially when the calf is so large, as this one was.

We could hear Willie cheerfully whistling away to himself in his workshop while we extracted a huge calf from the heifer. Thankfully it was alive and lively and so we returned to the job of suturing up the womb and the flank as rapidly as we could. It isn't too easy a task performing surgery under car headlights because a lot of the time, one's body is in the way of the light and one is suturing in a dark shadowy place.

The car headlights were beginning to become much dimmer as we finished putting in the last skin suture and as we did so, a beaming Willie appeared lugging a large tractor battery, a coil of wire and a light bulb.

"I've got a light rigged up!" He proudly announced. "You can start now."

"Ahem, we've just finished," we both said in unison! "Your calf is over there!"

"Oh, OK then. Thank you. I'll go and see to her."

"Good night, Willie, look after the calf. Phone us if there are any problems. See you again sometime!"

And so ended another calving! Fortunately, the car had enough battery power left to start the engine and we sped off back to our beds, laughing the whole while about Willie's attempts to be an electrician!

Never Underestimate People

It was a cold and windy winter's day, the sort of day that one would have quite happily not been outside in, but instead be inside in a nice cosy office. However, I had a job to do. As the newest member of the practice, I had been 'volunteered' to go and castrate some young calves for a rather taciturn, grumpy farmer; a man of few words it seemed who had a reputation for being short tempered and difficult! After a difference of opinion with another farmer the phrase 'well what do you expect from a pig but a grunt!' was uttered by his neighbour! Most farmers got on pretty well with their neighbours, but Jim Morrison was a man apart. He went to the market only when he absolutely needed to but otherwise never socialised with anyone.

So, with a certain amount of trepidation, I approached Jim's farm road, my ears still ringing with the words of my colleagues who had laughed about what an adventure my afternoon would be! Various old gates that were tied up with baler twine barred my way, but having successfully negotiated them, I arrived at his farmyard.

"Never seen you before!" was my greeting. "Must be new? Well, are you ready?" He added sharply and somewhat abruptly, "Let's get started."

I gathered my equipment from the car and followed him through what resembled a scrapyard of dead tractors and other rusting farm machinery, hoping that the afternoon might turn out rather better than I had anticipated. I held out little hope of getting the usual warm water, soap and a towel and I was proven to be absolutely correct! I was provided with an old, rusting bucket of tepid water, but that was about it! As I looked about, I could see that the 'handling' facilities were minimal and consisted of a few rusty old gates which were tied together with the ubiquitous baler twine.

"Where are the calves?" I asked and got a rather terse reply.

"That's them there," Jim said as he pointed to a group of sweating, snorting animals that were milling about inside an old farm building. I sighed inwardly as I looked at these 'calves' because they were about three times the size of what I had been expecting! Apparently, in an effort to save money he would only castrate his calves every second year so that there would be both yearlings and younger calves to attend to at the same time. Even the 'younger' calves were fairly old! Without any extra help, this could turn out to be an absolute rodeo, since the animals were not used to strangers and were even less enamoured about being housed!

I was tempted to say that these animals weren't exactly calves but thought that it would be prudent to hold my counsel, having been warned about Jim's somewhat intemperate personality! There was no choice but to just get on with the job in hand. At least, these young bulls were only needing to be castrated and fortunately didn't need de-horning as well. Notwithstanding that, this was highly likely to be an afternoon of getting bashed about by wild animals!

The sky was becoming darker and just as I was thinking that it could even begin to snow, I noticed a few flakes beginning to drift down. The afternoon was getting better and better!

One by one, the beasts were chased out of the building into the gated 'corral' (because he didn't own a cattle crush) and then they were trapped against the wall behind a gate that had been secured to the wall at one end by more baler twine. Every time we went near them, they lashed out with their back feet and some of their wilder moves could have got them walk-in parts in a Karate Kid movie! Whack, thump, bang they landed their blows with force and accuracy.

Fortunately, for me anyway, Jim Morrison was the recipient of most of them. I received my fair share of them too and I must admit that I was beginning to feel pretty battered and bruised. I made a determined effort to not react to the kicks and bashes because I didn't want to appear to be 'soft' on my first visit to the farm.

Jim uttered a few choice words as he shouted at his animals at times but I must admit that I was quite amazed at how resilient he was. It was an extremely cold day, and it was getting colder but he was dressed in trousers that had definitely seen better days and an old checked shirt that despite the cold, and occasional snowflakes, was wide open to the waist! He was on the receiving end of some pretty ferocious kicks from these half-grown bulls and yet he didn't seem to be at all bothered by them.

Although we didn't have lots of conversation, because we were busy, he did seem to become a bit more talkative, and I began to think he wasn't quite the really miserable, taciturn man that he had been described as. Maybe he was thawing because he was getting treated with respect, but I also suspected, and hoped, that he thought that I was doing a pretty good job in rather adverse conditions without complaining. Yes, the conditions were far from ideal, the handling equipment was lacking, and the animals were much older, crazier and bigger than they should have been, but I just kept quiet and worked away.

"Do you never feel the cold or the pain?" I asked him just after he had been the recipient of yet another powerful kick. I'm pretty certain that I winced for him!

Jim just stopped work for a minute and looked straight at me, his facial expression darkening and glowering.

"Pain!" he bellowed, "Pain! No! I never feel pain! Look at this face! Look at these hands! I don't feel pain anymore! Do you see them? Pain! See this nose, it is why I am so ugly." He said with great feeling as he then spat at the ground.

I was beginning to regret asking him!

I then looked closely at his face, and it was quite obvious that he wasn't blessed with film star looks! The main feature was his nose which was not only misshapen but was situated, rather oddly, towards one side of his face.

"See this nose! See this nose!" he said as he pointed to it. "This is what a Japanese soldier did to it. He smashed his rifle butt into my face and fractured it, moving my nose sideways! See these hands! Look at them, look at them! I have no fingernails! They were all pulled out by the Japanese when I was a POW in Changi! PAIN! I don't feel pain anymore," he raged at me. "There is no pain in this world that can come anywhere near that which they inflicted on me. Pain!" he said as he spat on the ground again. "Don't ever talk to me about pain!"

"Do you know?" he continued, "I left this farm to go to war, and with what I've seen of this world and its cruelty, I have no desire to ever leave it again! It holds nothing for me!"

Wow! I was suitably chastened and deeply affected by his story. This poor man had been through so much, so much more than I could ever have imagined! No wonder he was reclusive, and it seemed to me that the poor guy had been severely maligned by the local populace. I was left wondering exactly how many people had tried to get to know him or had heard his story. He wasn't asking for any sympathy; he was just relating what had happened to him!

He suddenly brightened up, almost as if he had shed a load of bottled-up stress and problems and he started being more chatty.

"How long have you been here?" he enquired.

"Three months," I replied, "I started after Mr Simpson died."

"Oh, I see! Now he really was a good vet," was the response. "He could cure anything you know. Great vet! He came here in my dad's time. Yes, he was a great vet!"

As we were manhandling the next beast into the catching arrangement behind a gate, we both were subject to more kicks. There were few farms on which the animals were so wild, and I was quite relieved there were only three left after this one. The wildest, most crazy, individuals, of course, always evaded capture until they were the only ones that were left!

"So, what made him such a great vet then?" I asked, as he tried to restrain a rather large animal.

As he grappled with the beast he replied, "He showed me how to hold a calf so that it can't kick."

"What did he teach you then?" I asked, somewhat bemused by his classification of the monster in front of us as a calf!

"Well, you put your left hand under his chin like this, pulling his head up, then take hold of his tail like this with your right hand and then you put your knee in his flank, like this, and then you've got him and he can't kick!"

As he was talking, I was standing behind the 'soon to be bullock' and was bending forward to take hold of the appropriate bits of anatomy before performing surgery on it. I went to grasp the bull's scrotum with my left hand, my scalpel in my right hand, listening to what he was saying to me.

No sooner had he uttered the words, "You've got him and he can't kick," did the animal give a jump and an almighty kick! The kick hit my left hand with such force that it caused my hand to fly backwards and to make contact with the scalpel blade in my right hand which was poised for surgery!

The end result was that my left thumb, palm and wrist were instantly incised to a significant depth, with tendons, veins, arteries and flesh exposed. It wasn't exposed for long though, because copious amounts of blood soon obscured the view! Fortunately, by some miracle I could still move and feel my fingers.

Having listened to Jim's suffering and his ability to bear pain, I felt obliged just to carry on and castrate the animal in front of me! I couldn't be a wimp. This was rapidly, if not somewhat awkwardly, accomplished and I stood up to take stock of the situation. My hand was running with blood and the bucket of disinfectant had now turned into the colour of an expensive red wine! If I didn't get the haemorrhage arrested soon then I would lose a substantial and significant amount of blood.

There weren't many animals left to do but it was quite apparent that I needed to stop the blood and then get my hand wound sutured up. I wasn't going to be defeated at this point by a hand injury and so I returned to my car to get a pad of gauze and after covering the wound with it, I donned two pairs of surgical gloves in an attempt to put pressure on the wound to stem the bleeding. It was more annoying than painful because I knew that my hand would be awkward to use for quite a few days, until it had healed.

I returned to the task and castrated another bull calf. *Only one to go*, I thought to myself, with considerable relief, that is until I looked at my hand! The surgical gloves were still in place but the fingers, of what were actually quite tight-fitting gloves, were gradually elongating in front of my eyes and were now twice as long as they should be and were filled with blood! My blood! Hmmm. I needed to get this bleeding stopped quickly. The last animal was castrated, and I have to say it was a very awkward procedure because of the long blood-filled fingers on the gloves.

After washing my wellies and clinical coat etc., I removed the gloves and with Jim's help, applied a bandage and a new glove.

"You need to get that hand fixed, lad," he said. "I'll open the gates and let you out. Thanks for your help today. Mr Simpson couldn't have done it better!"

Wow! Praise indeed! I decided that Jim Morrison wasn't so bad after all!

So, off I drove with my left hand held high above my head height in an attempt to slow the bleeding. It obviously wasn't going to stop, and I reckoned that I could manage to drive the 10 miles or so to the local doctors to get sutured up before I had totally exsanguinated!

Steering with one hand and changing gear with the 'wrong hand' was awkward but I drove off as safely as I could with my bandaged hand in the air!

There are no secrets in the farming community and word gets around fairly quickly as to where the vets are and which farms, they would be visiting on their rounds. This enabled some of the more tight-fisted farmers to never request a 'call out' but to waylay the vets between the farms that they were already visiting and thus only get charged for a 'passing visit'! Much cheaper!

As I carefully made my way down the lane from Jim's farm, heading to the local doctor's, I was aware of a tractor, with its headlamps flashing, careering across the fields of the neighbouring farm. It dawned on me that the driver was trying to intercept my journey since he was wildly waving his cap as he leaned out of the cab. *Oh no, what now?* I thought! I slowed down and stopped as the farmer got out the cab. It was Donald, the farmer from the next-door dairy farm.

"I'm so glad that I caught you, I've got a lame coo. Think she's got an abscess in her foot. Could you just nip in by and sort her, seeing as you're passing? I've been watching for you leaving since I saw you going up to that miserable sod next door earlier on."

I showed him my bandaged and gloved hand that I was holding in the air. "I'm very sorry, I've got a pretty bad hand injury that needs suturing. I'm afraid that you will need to phone the surgery and get someone else out."

My response was met with a grimace and a grunt because he obviously was neither too pleased, nor by the look on his face was he too convinced of the seriousness of my injury. Young people nowadays weren't as hardy as they used to be! Moreover, it was now going to cost him more money than he intended paying!

I managed to get the car back into gear and slowly drove off towards the main road and I must admit that I was beginning to feel a bit weak and lightheaded. Instead of my usual high-speed dash along the main road I had to make a determined effort to concentrate and to drive at a sedate pace. My hand continued to bleed through the bandage and after about 10 miles it was with considerable relief that I reached our surgery premises.

"My goodness, you're as white as a sheet! What's happened to you?" was my greeting from the receptionists. "Right! We are phoning Dr McLeod and you can just get yourself along there to get it fixed."

Fortunately, I only had about another mile and a half to drive to his surgery. It was either that or drive 30 miles to the nearest A and E hospital!

Dr McLeod gave me some local anaesthetic, which was more painful to endure than the original laceration! I didn't really think that his decision to use black, silk sutures was exactly ideal, but I was in no position to question him. I was just grateful to get the bleeding stopped and to get my hand resurrected!

Of course, as fate would have it, I was 'on call' that night and had to attend to a cow calving! Not an ideal way of nursing a sutured hand. The next day, too, it was work as normal, digging about in cows' hooves, removing decomposing afterbirths and performing all the usual duties of a large animal vet.

It was, therefore, no great surprise when a few days later my hand became red, hot and swollen and all the sutures burst open! Release of the sutures and the purulent discharge afforded enormous relief and eventually, in about two weeks, my hand had fully healed!

I was left to reflect upon how fortunate I had been to have not sustained a more serious injury. Another millimetre or so and I would have been left with no hand function! At least there was no nerve damage and no tendon injuries!

The most positive result of the saga was that I had experienced a valuable lesson in the handling of pain and injuries and that one must never judge a person's character when you don't know anything about them! Jim Morrison was a unique character but his attitude to pain was amazing, and I think that coloured my own perception of how to handle pain and injuries during my career. Injuries, bites, bruises, fractured limbs or ribs can be extremely painful, but how you handle the pain is what really matters.

I, fortunately, would never experience the horrors of a POW camp and thus I realised that nothing that I may experience in the future could ever equate to the pain that Jim had endured. Therefore, things might be painful at times but with a positive attitude one could quickly discount the pain and just get on with living with whatever injury had been incurred! Injuries may be physical, but the degree of pain perception is definitely in one's own mind!

If Only They Couldn't Talk!

As everyone knows, parrots can be amazing mimics and are reputed to have the intelligence of a 4 to 5-year old child. They are certainly very talented birds. Many are expert at reproducing not only accurate interpretations of voices and accents but also the sounds of inanimate objects such as phones, car alarms and the beep of smoke alarms that need new batteries!

The first thing that a bird stops doing when it becomes unwell is that it stops vocalising and it becomes very quiet. Conversely, as it recovers and begins to feel better its speech is the last thing to return. Together with other parameters the return of speech was a good guide as to when birds were ready to go home. When the nurses uncovered the birds' cages first thing in the morning, it was not unusual for the nurse's cheery greeting to the parrot of 'Good Morning' to be answered with an expletive such as 'F...k Off!' or from the more polite ones 'Want toast, Want toast. Will you hurry up!' These were patients that were quite obviously now ready to go home!

One had to be extremely careful when talking in front of the birds because they would pick up words and repeat them at a later stage. One bird, after returning home, managed to drive its owners daft by constantly making a beeping sound which it had copied from some of the instrumentation/monitoring equipment in the practice! Staff needed to be careful with their language because even on the rare occasions that they got nipped or bitten the parrot would not only repeat 'Ouch' or similar but also add in more 'expressive' words when it got home! One amazon parrot used to try and bite the staff and before they could react it would say, "Ouch ya b…r! You are such a bad bird!"

The first occasion, that I can really remember when I realised how amazing African Greys, in particular, could be at copying sounds, was when I was doing a house visit to examine a cat. After I had dealt with the cat, the owner and I started discussing the parrot and she told me how brilliant it was at mimicking sounds, let alone human voices.

"Just watch this!" she said as she proceeded to go into the kitchen and to call the cat through for some food. The cat was a large, fluffy white Persian called Avalanche.

"Avalanche come and get your dinner," she called to the cat whilst banging on the cat's food tin with a spoon.

Avalanche looked up, got up, stretched and then ambled over towards the kitchen. Just as she reached the door the parrot shouted, "Avalanche. Come and get your dinner!" and made the exact noise of a food tin being hit with a spoon! Avalanche stopped and turned back towards the parrot's cage appearing totally confused! If a cat with her amazingly sensitive hearing can be confused by a parrot, then it demonstrates just how accurate a parrot can be as a mimic, or perhaps it just showed that Avalanche wasn't a very bright cat!

A rather distressed gentleman arrived for an appointment together with his African Grey parrot, Roger, who wasn't very well at all. Roger had stopped talking and was sitting looking rather miserable and 'fluffed up' on the perch in is cage. Apparently, when Roger was 'his usual self' he was the most amazing talker and his talents had brought him a career in TV and in films which was quite lucrative for his owner!

Roger was afflicted by a serious respiratory infection which, if not treated in time, was highly likely to be life threatening!

"How long will he take to get better?" asked his concerned owner, Mr Black. "Will I need to leave him with you? Oh dear! This is really worrying. He is so precious and I am so attached to him. Do you think that he will get better?"

"His only chance of getting better is if we admit him for intensive treatment with drugs and nebulisation. Sadly, without that, yes, he is likely to get worse and die," I replied.

"Oh, my goodness! I do wish that I had brought him sooner! Will he need to be in for long?" was the next question followed by, "I have to go away soon to Japan for a few weeks, will he be better before I go?"

"When do you go?" I asked him. "It will be quite a few days before we can tell if he is improving, and he may need treatment for a few weeks after that."

"I'm going next week and I will be away for four weeks or so. Can you keep him until I get back?"

That was a difficult request since we had limited space and a constant throughput of sick parrots. We came to an arrangement that once Roger had finished his initial treatment then he would go to a lady, locally, who boarded parrots as well as dogs and cats. However, he would only leave Roger if I promised to communicate with him every night while he was away and after he had met the lady with the boarding kennels first. Having met the lady and with her getting his approval, he finally agreed to leave Roger with us! His final request was that Roger was never to hear anybody using bad language since he had an incredible talent for picking up new words and if he started swearing then that might be the end of his film and TV appearances!

"Ok, that's not a problem, there's no swearing goes on in here," I told him. "Once Roger has improved, I will take him up to the boarding kennels and I will warn them about their language too!"

Roger, fortunately, recovered fairly quickly and started speaking again. Mr Black was absolutely correct. Roger was an extremely talented bird that could chat away to the staff and was also able to burst into song too! He particularly liked to strike up some sort of conversation when the telephone was being answered, usually trying, in his own noisy way, to compete with the caller or maybe he was trying to outdo the person who was answering the phone in the surgery.

Whatever the reason, he caused a lot of amusement and we weren't looking forward to the day when he would be leaving us. Well, that was the case until the day that I had to tell a client that her 19 years old cat had sadly died. Her pet had terminal renal failure and wasn't expected to get better and of course, the inevitable happened and he passed away. It is never an easy phone call to make when one has to tell a client that their pet has died and we always tried to be empathetic, sympathetic and to deal with the situation with gentility and compassion.

"I am absolutely and utterly disgusted! I have never heard anything like it!" was the response to my phone call. I must admit that I was somewhat taken aback by the client's indignation because she had been well warned that the end for her cat was not only inevitable but was imminent too and I pointed this out to her. She didn't want euthanasia for her cat but had requested every possible step to keep him alive and comfortable.

"Yes, I knew that he was going to die and I had come to terms with that. What I'm complaining about is that my dear old cat has just died and you are phoning me up with the sad news when there is, quite obviously, a lot of hilarity going on in your office. In fact, I am certain that you're having a party! It is absolutely terrible. It is disgusting! I really can't believe you could be so insensitive."

"There is most certainly no party going on here," I replied.

"Well, what exactly is that noise then?" was the rejoinder.

I was so engrossed in my phone call that I hadn't been aware of Roger who was in full voice in the background! He was singing and shouting, as he often did when someone was on the phone. "Are you all alright there? Ha, ha, ha. How's it going? Oh my, you are pretty! Give us a kiss, etc.," Accompanied by outburst of even more raucous laughter!

"Oh, I'm so sorry. I didn't realise. That's a parrot that you can hear in the background."

"A parrot? Don't give me that! Parrots don't make that sort of noise. I know that you're having a party and I'm thoroughly disgusted and totally disappointed!" and with that she rang off!

Roger had a wide-ranging vocabulary and apart from that one incident he provided us with a lot of amusement and entertainment. I reported on his progress every night to his owner, including the fact that he hadn't learnt any bad words!

The time came for Roger to move off for the rest of his recuperation at the boarding kennels and I suddenly remembered to warn the kennel owner that he must never hear any swearing, otherwise his career might be finished! She was also instructed to phone me every night to let me know how he was getting on so that I could then let his owner know, who by this time was in Japan.

"OK, then, I will keep Roger in the house and I suppose that I had better warn my husband because his language can be a bit fruity at times!"

Her husband was a cockney who had also served in the Royal Navy and I had memories of his colourful vocabulary! I suspected that it might, indeed, be quite a difficult task for him to reign in his language!

Every night I got the obligatory phone call from the boarding kennels about Roger, and every evening I relayed the news to his owner. I never failed to ask if he had learnt any bad words too!

On the final evening before he was due to go home, Mrs Moore phoned me about Roger and she sounded a bit tense.

"What's wrong?" I asked her. "Is Roger OK?"

"Well, er, yes he's fine," she said, but I noticed a slight hesitation in her voice.

"Oh no! Please don't tell me that he's started swearing?" I asked her with some amount of trepidation.

"Er, well not exactly," was her answer. "It's just that every time the telephone rings now he has started shouting at the top of his voice, 'Would you just shut that "bladdy" parrot up!' in my husband's cockney voice!"

Although parrots are great mimics, it is sometimes difficult to actually work out just how intelligent they are. I have often dwelt on the fact that they always use words in appropriate situations but I have sometimes been absolutely astounded at the 'conversations' that they can have.

I remember visiting a client's house where there were a number of parrots of different species, some which spoke and some which didn't. As I was leaving, she said, "Come and listen to this," and we stood quietly outside an indoor aviary which housed three birds. The amazing thing to listen to was them conversing in human language!

"Who is a pretty boy then?"…parrot one.

"Give us a kiss?"…parrot two.

"Ooh, you are awful!" replied parrot three!

One would have thought that they would have just used bird language when there were no humans about! That situation, however, was not that uncommon because sometime later three Amazon parrots, all from the same household, had come in for some surgical biopsy procedures and were waiting to be collected. For no particular reason, one of them started singing the children's song 'Old Macdonald had a Farm' and then the other two joined in with it and they went through the whole repertoire of alternately making the various farm animal noises! Perfectly in tune too! Clients who were in the waiting room were convinced that we had a primary school class in for a visit and that the children were singing!

A regular client, Mrs Macintosh, who owned a few talented birds, 'rescued' an Amazon parrot and caged it in her living room along with her other birds. She was in the kitchen when she heard a voice coming from the bird's room and so she sidled over to the door and carefully peered round the corner. One of the African Greys was saying, "Go on, go on, go on," which she didn't understand until she looked further into the room and saw the 'new' bird starting to strip the wallpaper next to its cage. The African Grey parrot was encouraging it by saying "Go on! Go on!" and then just as it stripped a large amount of paper off the wall it added, "Ooh! You are a bad bird! We will need to find you a new home!"

It was then that she realised that she used to say that phrase to her African Grey when it was younger and it had added the words to its own repertoire and used them appropriately!

Towards the end of an evening consulting time, I received a phone call from that same lady. She was in an absolute panic because one of her Macaws had almost bitten the beak right off one of her husband's favourite birds, a little conure, and it was losing a lot of blood. She was advised to bring it in straight away and that I would wait for her.

A short time later she arrived, together with her husband, who was gently cradling an extremely dejected conure whose face was covered in blood and whose beak was still attached to its face but was sitting at a strange angle. "I think we may be too late," sighed the husband. "Mutley has lost a lot of blood and he's pretty limp now."

"We need to admit him and get some fluids and first aid treatment into him if he is to survive. He may need a blood transfusion. You will need to leave him with us."

"Oh! I don't want to do that. He's never been away from me and I don't want him to die in here!" wailed Mr Macintosh.

"I'm sorry but you have no choice. Take him home and he will definitely die! I'm going to put him into an incubator immediately while we get some treatment sorted," I told him.

"I'm afraid there are no guarantees of survival. I will give you a phone later tonight and then if he is still with us, you can give us a call in the morning and we'll see how he gets on."

Well, Mutley struggled to hold his own but he survived the night but still was extremely weak and could only sit on the floor of the incubator. He wasn't strong enough to perch. I felt that it was still a 'touch and go' situation!

Mr Macintosh came to visit Mutley after he had finished his work the next evening and I told him that he still wasn't very well and that his survival wasn't assured. He looked at Mutley who never responded when he spoke to the bird and just sat all fluffed up on the floor of the incubator.

"I'm taking him home," announced Mr Macintosh. "If he's going to die, he can die in his own home. I can't leave him here again. Yes, he's coming home." And with that he lifted Mutley up and put him on the perch in his travelling cage.

"Well, on your own head be it then!" I replied, "I definitely can't agree with it but I can't stop you if those are your wishes. You can take him on condition that you keep him really, really warm and that if he survives then you bring him back tomorrow. You aren't giving him his best chance you know?"

"He will die if I leave him. He needs to be with me!"

"I'll put the car heater on high and I will drive him home as fast as I can!" and with that Mr Macintosh rushed out with Mutley barely clinging to his perch. I must admit that I was rather sad because we had worked feverishly overnight to keep him alive and now, he had a good chance of dying!

The next evening Mr Macintosh appeared with the travelling cage and lo and behold Mutley was sitting on the perch within it, still looking ill, but he was alive and definitely appearing a lot brighter.

"Wow! He's alive! I didn't really think he would make it when you took him away last night!"

"Well, to tell you the truth I didn't think that he would either!" replied Mr Macintosh. "I had the car heated up and I set off at great speed to get him home. As I careered round the first sharp bend, just down the road there, I heard a bang as Mutley fell off his perch! *Oh no!* I thought, he has died and the vet was correct! I stopped the car, put the interior light on and looked into his cage and as I stared at his lifeless body, he suddenly shook himself, looked at me and he said, 'You Bastard!' I just knew he was going to be OK then! That was my boy! I am afraid that he swears like a navvy!"

Mrs Macintosh was hugely embarrassed by her husband's bird and its language but Mutley recovered and got back to his normal swearing self!

One of the most impressive parrots from the point of view of 'intelligent' talking was an African Grey parrot which came in for an examination one day. It was a really tame, confident individual that didn't seem to be at all nervous about being in a strange place. I spoke to it and gently took it out of its cage and wrapped it in a towel so that I could examine it. While I was listening to its heart with my stethoscope, I was aware that it was speaking so I took the stethoscope out of my ears and said to the owner, "Did he say something there?"

I had no sooner asked the question when the parrot said, "What are you doing this to me for?"

To say that I was astounded was a bit of understatement! The owner informed me that the parrot loved visiting the vets and liked the attention.

"Well, he's probably not going to like the next bit because I'm going to take a blood sample from him!"

"He won't mind!" was the reply and as I prepared the syringe and he caught sight of it he let out a loud, excited, "Whoo-hoo!"

I took his blood sample without any resistance or objection from him. As I put the bird back on the table, he stood up straight, shook the towel off his shoulders, looked at me and said, "Is that it then?" and climbed back into his cage! I must admit that I was totally amazed and still find it hard to believe!

On the other hand, I'm pretty certain that many owners sometimes have occasion to regret that their parrots can speak! It was not uncommon to have parrots coming out with the most foul language when they were away from home. Most times, their owners would blame an old uncle or husband who had been at sea and who had developed some pretty bad ways of expressing themselves! The problem for them was that the parrots swore in the exact voice and accent of their owners, many of whom were otherwise very demure little ladies; well at least that was the impression that they gave to the outside world! You little b…r or get me an f…g cup of tea was some of the phrases heard! "Say that again and I'll knock your f…g lights out you b…d," was a bit more disconcerting!

However, many birds weren't offensive but were just highly amusing! One regular visitor belonged to a man who was a football fanatic. His bird and he were absolutely inseparable! The parrot, Smokey, used to sit on his shoulder while he was watching football matches on the TV. Smokey, apparently, became as involved in the games as its owner and was often heard to join in shouts of 'goal!' or even to hurl abuse at the referee such as, "where are your f...g specs!" His wife tolerated the bird but had no real affection for it since it didn't really like her, a not uncommon situation in many households!

"Where's your husband today?" I asked her on one occasion when I met her.

"He's off work just now with an injury and so he's a bit housebound," she replied and added, "and anyway I'm not speaking to him just now! He just sits there watching the TV all day with that feathered thing sitting on his shoulder! Do you know that I was out shopping the other day and when I arrived home and opened the door, I distinctly heard 'IT' say 'Here's the old witch back!'"

They can only repeat what they have heard but it is amazing how often people buy a hand-reared bird and then come to the vets for a check-up, shortly after purchase, and complain that it isn't speaking! I assume that they must think that they come pre-programmed to talk! Like children, they need to learn to speak as they develop and grow.

One man, who I will never forget, arrived with his newly acquired African Grey parrot for a post purchase check-up. It was only about 4 months of age but he was one of those of the 'it isn't speaking yet' brigade. There must be something wrong with it! Of course, there was nothing physically wrong with the bird, it was just too young to talk! Like human beings, some individuals are more talented than others when it comes to speech and some birds never do anything but whistle. Some owners, too, are much more able than others at teaching their birds to talk and the good ones invariably get their birds to speak well.

This client, however, wasn't in the talented group of teachers and without being too unkind was somewhat deficient in the speech and intelligence departments himself! Every month he would return with his parrot to complain that it wasn't talking yet! Telling him to be patient and informing him that some birds were more talented than others was a waste of time. He'd bought a parrot and he expected it to talk! End of story!

After 18 months he appeared as usual, not to complain about the bird not speaking but to request that it was put to sleep! He had just had enough of it and it was driving him absolutely demented! We never 'put birds to sleep' and most times if they had problems, we would rehome them to more suitable environments, or on occasion I would take them home myself until any problems were sorted out. Enquiring further about his issues with the bird it turned out that he spent all day watching war films with the bird, sitting on the back of his armchair, watching the films with him.

Being a bit of a loner, that was his whole life! Unfortunately, the parrot, being an accurate mimic had started imitating the noises that it heard on the TV screen and incessantly made the noises of falling/exploding bombs or bullets ricocheting! Wheeeeee! Bang! Wheeee! Roar, bang wallop, accompanied by a high-pitched whistle as the imaginary bombs fell and this was repeated constantly all day! It was difficult not to feel extremely sorry for the client because he had very little else in his life apart from the war films and his parrot and a precarious state of mental health!

One of the down sides of taking parrots home to rehabilitate them was that, from time to time, it caused my neighbours some surprises. In the warmer weather, I put them in outdoor aviaries in the garden. One of our neighbours was out hanging her washing, attired in her night clothes, when as she stretched up to peg some item of clothing on the line, she heard a shrill 'wolf whistle' coming from the direction of our garden. It startled her somewhat but didn't really phase her too much since she thought that she was getting some, not unwelcome, male admiration! However, that all changed when a deep male voice started talking to her over the hedge and thinking she was about to be molested, she ran for the safety of her house! The 'voice', of course, and the whistle came from one of the parrots in our garden!

I have always been amazed and impressed how some people can get budgies to talk and one particular budgie I will never forget! This bird was extremely well loved and as it aged, he began to develop arthritis in his feet and leg joints. His owners were totally devoted to the little bird and they had fashioned wider perches for him which they had covered in a soft velvety material to try and make his perching more comfortable. The reason for needing to examine Joey on this occasion was because he had developed quite severe diarrhoea. He was 10 years of age and was seriously unwell.

"I'm afraid that Joey will need to come in for investigation and intensive treatment if he is to be given the best chance of survival. He is really extremely ill," I informed her.

"Oh no!" was her distressed reply. "Joey is just so precious and talented. I do honestly believe that he is the most talented budgerigar in the country! Do you know that he has a one-hundred-word vocabulary?"

No pressure here then, I thought to myself as I looked at Joey sitting all fluffed up on the bottom of the cage. "He definitely needs to come in immediately for some fluids and intensive care or we will lose him."

Mrs Martin was none too happy at having to leave Joey with me. "He's our family you know? We don't have any children. Oh! Please do your best for him. I am so worried. Could you ring me later and let me know how he is, please?"

As it turned out, Joey slowly improved but he needed to be hospitalised for 3 days. On the third day, he started cheeping and being vocal and so we knew that he was definitely on the mend and could probably go home.

I telephoned Mrs Martin and told her that Joey had started being noisy again and that he was able to return home.

"Oh! How fantastic!" Mrs Martin trilled down the phone. "You've heard him speaking! I told you he was a great talker!"

"Well," I replied, "he was just making budgie noises."

"What did you say? Budgie noises? Don't give me that! Joey doesn't do budgie noises!" was her indignant reply.

I let that topic of conversation stop and arranged for her to come and collect him later that day.

Ushering her into the consulting room I could feel her excitement at being reunited with Joey. She almost pushed me aside as she rushed in, leaving the door open behind her. "Where's Joey?" she enquired.

"I will just go and get him for you. Just give me a second," as I went to get him.

I returned with Joey, in his cage, who was now sitting on the velvet-covered perch and looking quite perky!

Mrs Martin was beside herself with excitement and as she put her face right up to the cage she said, "Mummy has missed you so much! So how IS my little Joey?" and almost immediately, in a voice that was crystal clear and as loud as a human who was speaking, he replied, "Joey Martin's got dirty wee jobbies!"

There were guffaws of laughter from the people in the waiting room who had clearly heard the budgie talking! I could hardly keep my face straight too for it was obvious that Joey really was an extremely good and clear speaker!

Mrs Martin's face flushed with embarrassment as she tried to explain. "Oh dear! I'm afraid that is my fault! Every day, when I came home from work and when he had his diarrhoea, I used to look in the bottom of his cage and say, 'Who has got dirty wee jobbies then?' He must have remembered!"

Poor woman then had to exit with the cage through the laughing clientele in the waiting room! At least she had demonstrated that he was, indeed, an amazing talker and for his part, Joey had added some new words to his already extensive vocabulary!

Veterinary surgeons, as one would of course expect, totally concentrate on the animals that are brought to them and never, ever notice the often extremely attractive ladies who bring them in!

Buttons was the most handsome, cuddly tame cockatoo that one could ever imagine. He had been hand-reared and was an absolute delight to handle. He usually arrived at the surgery with the lady that owned him together with her two children and it was quite obvious that they absolutely adored him. Mrs MacKay had obtained him as a baby and he had been hand-reared. He loved everybody until he reached about 4 years of age when his male hormones began to manifest their presence! A common feature of sexually mature birds is that they prefer humans of the opposite gender and can actively dislike those of the same gender as themselves. Children are never perceived as 'love' rivals and are therefore tolerated!

The Mackay household transitioned into a hotbed of cockatoo hormones where Buttons went from regarding Mrs Mackay as his mum to claiming her as his wife! It all started quite casually when, if Mr Mackay sat down on the settee too close to his wife, Buttons would nip him with his beak! This then progressed to the situation where the couple couldn't sit close together at all and so they had to occupy different ends of the settee! Buttons, however, became more and more possessive and, indeed, aggressive towards Mr Mackay and would run across the settee and bite him hard!

He must have been a very tolerant husband because he then accepted that he couldn't sit near his wife and took to relaxing in an armchair on the other side of the room. However, Buttons wasn't so tolerant of his love rival and began flying across the room to actively attack Mr Mackay!

Buttons' behaviour deteriorated considerably but instead of maybe keeping him locked in his cage when Mr Mackay was about, he was still allowed his freedom to cuddle with the rest of the family. Perhaps that was a better alternative than listening to the ear-splitting screeching of a caged amorous, and extremely jealous, cockatoo! The situation had become so bad that Mr Mackay had taken to wearing a motorbike crash helmet before entering the house when he arrived home! It was the only safe way of protecting himself from the ferocity of Button's attacks!

Buttons had progressed from nipping and biting his love rival to trying to disable him by ripping his beak off!

Commonly known in human terminology as a nose! Being bitten by a cockatoo means sustaining one of the of the worst bird-bite injuries since their lower beaks have a V shaped notch that the upper mandible neatly locks into, ensuring that they give a painful bite and with which they can efficiently attach themselves to their victim!

I had met Buttons on a number of previous occasions and, as always when away from his territory, he was a delightful character.

"You have to help me!" sobbed Mrs Mackay. "This darling bird is wrecking my home and my marriage and I don't know what to do. Please! You have got to do something for us!" she pleaded and then related the story of the bird's increasing aggression at home, finishing with the crash helmet saga! "It has got so bad that something has got to be done because my husband is finding it so difficult to live with Buttons now and the rest of us don't want to part with the bird. He's just our baby."

She then began sobbing again, and I was forced to look at her and 'somehow' noticed that she was an extremely attractive woman! Buttons was obviously a bit like 'MR KIPLING' and had exceedingly good taste, in his choice of a potential mate! I could see where he was coming from because she was quite stunning! Mrs Mackay had the biggest, darkest blue eyes that I had ever seen and as I looked at her, I could see big tears beginning to form, which made her lovely eyes look even bigger!

"Is it really that bad?" I asked her. "Has it got to the stage of either you keep the bird or your husband?"

"Y-Y-Yes, it's that bad! It has got to that stage!" she replied as she wailed and sobbed even more.

Realising that she was extremely upset and that I probably had been a bit blunt with my questioning, I thought that I would lighten the atmosphere by teasing her a little.

"Is it a difficult decision then?" I enquired. "Is it a question of whether you either keep Buttons or your husband?"

Sadly, this prompted renewed sobbing! "N-N-No," she stammered. "It's not difficult, it's an easy decision." Then she paused and continued, "It's just that the bird doesn't bring in a wage!"

The final result was that Buttons was given a hormonal implant and sent to a 'boot camp' for a couple of months until his behaviour and hormones settled. Mr Mackay was able to dispense with his crash helmet and Buttons had to spend a lot of his time in an aviary. Marriage saved!

End of Life Services

As Great Danes go, Charlotte, was one of the biggest and she belonged to a lovely couple who were long-standing family friends, the Robbs. She had led a healthy, pampered life but like many dogs of her breed was not destined to have a long life. The time came for her to depart this earth when she was no longer able to get about easily and was unable to live her life without constant pain.

I arrived at Charlotte's (Charley's) home and she was carefully and gently given an injection so that she slipped away 'to sleep' in the arms of her grieving owners. The euthanasia was straightforward but I then began to be concerned about how I was going to manage to remove such a big dog for the usual canine cremation. So, it was with considerable relief that Mr Robb said, "I wonder if you would mind giving me a hand to move her from the living room here out into the garden? I have decided to bury her at her favourite spot where she used to lie when the weather was warm."

"Absolutely, I would be delighted to do that," I replied, whilst inwardly whooping with delight that I wasn't going to have to try and carry her to my car. Phew, that was a relief! We carefully rolled Charley onto a blanket and dragged her out into the garden because even between the two of us, Mr

Robb seemingly not being particularly strong, she was difficult to move.

"I have started to dig her grave," he said as we traversed the lawn, "but I have hurt my ribs and I am finding it really difficult to do anything just now. It is over there under the apple tree. Would you mind burying her for us?"

At that, my heart sank because his attempts at a grave had ended up with a large area that had been dug to the great depth of about two inches! Worse than that, it was under an old apple tree.

"I decided to bury her here because it was her favourite spot and it means that I can still look out of the window when I am working and see her grave," was the explanation.

I had no choice but to remove my jacket and start digging! If you have ever tried to dig at all under an apple tree then you will perhaps realise what I was up against because there were stout roots spreading everywhere! It took me forever, or so it seemed and the deeper that I dug, the more robust the tree roots became. My back was aching and I was having difficulty making more progress with the grave and so I decided that Charley would just have to be buried in a shallow grave! So, I gently and with dignity lowered (not very far!) the dog's body into the grave, being acutely aware that I was being watched from the house! Normally, graves for animals are a few feet deep but this one could probably be more accurately measured in inches! Anyway, I was unable to dig anymore since I was recovering from broken ribs myself and so I started filling in the 'grave'.

I didn't exactly stand back to admire my finished handiwork but I must admit that in retrospect the grave and final interment probably bore more resemblance to a Great Dane shaped mole hill rather than a traditional burial site!

Exhausted and unable to stand up straight because of my aching back and ribs I made my way to my car, vowing never to get involved in burying a dog ever again!

"Mrs Mitchell wants you to call in on your way home tonight to put her dog Hector to sleep. He can't walk anymore and she thinks that his time has come," the receptionist informed me.

I sighed, for it had been a particularly harrowing, busy day and it was now after 8:00 p.m. and I was tired and hungry. Attending to Hector was the last thing that I felt like doing that evening, not least because he was a hugely overweight, spoilt Doberman who just didn't like me at all!

However, I had known Mrs Mitchell for a long time, and I knew that there was no way that she would have been able to manage to bring Hector to the surgery, because he was unable to walk anymore.

It was a typical November night with cold lashing rain, in fact it had been raining like that all day, and of course it was a pitch-black night too. I ran up the drive to her house as quickly as I could in a rather futile attempt to stay dry.

"Oh, I am so glad that you have come. Poor Hector, he hasn't been able to get up all day and taking into account all his other problems, I really think that it is time for him to go. We will miss him dreadfully. I am so upset but thank you so much for coming out tonight because I really just couldn't bear to watch him any longer."

I followed Mrs Mitchell into her dining room to be greeted by her old father who was sitting by an open fire. "It's a rotten night," he observed and then pointed to the dining table. "The old boy's under there."

The 'Old Boy', Hector couldn't be seen because the table was adorned with a lace edged, heavy table covering that reached right down to the ground on all sides! They requested that I just attended to him where he lay because neither of them was fit to get him out and, of course, he couldn't walk anymore. I sighed inwardly because I knew that my only option was to get under the tablecloth and do what was needed to be done under there! Not the easiest of situations to carry out an efficient euthanasia.

I lifted the bottom of the lacy cloth and looked under the table to be greeted with a low, throaty growl from Hector who was simultaneously curling his lips and showing his dirty, yellow teeth! "Oh! This is just fantastic," I muttered silently to myself while Mrs Mitchell was saying, "Oh please! Don't upset the poor boy." That was going to be a difficult request to fulfil since Hector's dislike of me seemed to have considerably increased along with his waistline! I suppose, after all, I was the intruder into his home and so his growling was slightly understandable.

Euthanasia was to be carried out by an injection into a vein of his foreleg, somewhere, unfortunately, that wasn't too far from the bared teeth! I summoned up all my courage and by a tremendous feat of daring, hoping Hector did not try to bite me, I clipped his foreleg, raised the vein and administered his injection. Although I was totally concentrating on not getting bitten by Hector, I was also aware of a running monologue from Mrs Mitchell, who was standing by the fireside and who was totally unable to see what was going on under the table because the cloth had fallen down behind me!

"Please. Please don't hurt him! Be a good boy now, Hector, for Mr Alexander, he is just trying to help you. Oh! Please don't upset him and be gentle with him!" The last comment being addressed to me rather than Hector!

Hector, fortunately didn't get the satisfaction of sinking his teeth into me and he slipped away peacefully, the growls fading as he slept away. I reversed out from under the table and stood up, rather stiffly, because I had been lying in a really uncomfortable and somewhat awkward position under the table and across the old fashioned, crossed table legs!

As, I packed away the syringes and drugs back into my medical case Mrs Mitchell had one last request. "Would you mind burying the poor old soul for us?" she asked in a pleading voice.

What choice did I have? I couldn't just leave him under the table, and I could see that neither the overweight Mrs Mitchell nor her 90 years old father were capable of lifting him. I had promised myself that I would never, ever help to bury another dog and Mrs Mitchell must have seen the expression on my face for she said, "Oh. It's OK. You don't have to bury him; I got the gardener to dig his grave earlier on today when I knew his end was near. Would you just be kind enough to just carry him to his grave and lay him in it for us, please?"

Well, that was a request that I could hardly refuse, and it didn't seem that it would be quite as difficult a procedure as the Great Dane burial was! The real problem that I was faced with was getting Hector out from underneath the table in a dignified manner, and then actually being able to lift him off the ground for he had added even more weight to his considerable mass since I had last seen him! I looked at him lying there. He was huge and carrying him would have even challenged a Mr Universe competitor!

I knew that if I didn't remove my jacket that I would split the seam at the back and so I took it off, even though it meant carrying Hector out into the rainstorm that was going on outside! With a struggle I pulled Hector out from under the table, which in itself was difficult because of the obstructions caused by the crossed members of the table legs.

Once he was finally out, I wrapped him in the rug from his bed and then attempted to lift the hugely overweight dog. The only way that I could possibly manage this feat was to squat down and somehow get him onto my knees, then after a slight pause, to try and stand up using every ounce of the power in my thighs!

Having now reached a standing position, I headed for the back door because I knew that I couldn't carry his weight for very long! Mrs Mitchell was busy putting on her wellies and raincoat and was searching for an umbrella too!

"Open the door, and quickly," I shouted to her. "He is really heavy and I can't hold onto him for too long." She heard the urgency in my voice and managed to hop to the door with one wellington on so that she could open it. I dashed out into the night, which, as anticipated, was an extremely wet one, and started off towards the garden.

"Wait for me," was all I heard as I hurried to get Hector interred before I dropped him! "I can't find my umbrella." It had been raining heavily all day and the rear garden lawn was like an Olympic skating rink because of the clay soil that was a feature of that area. I therefore had extreme difficulty slipping and sliding up the incline that was her back lawn. I reached the top of the slope and then saw that I was going to have to negotiate an even more hazardous descent to the bottom of the garden! As I slipped and slid on the clay soil, I could hear Mrs Mitchell close the back door of her house and start to climb up the initial slope. "I'm coming, wait for me," was all that I heard. By this time, not only was I absolutely drenched by the heavy rain but I could also feel Hector getting heavier and heavier and beginning to slip out of my grasp.

"Where is the grave?" I shouted over my shoulder. "I can't see it!"

"It's in the corner at the bottom of the slope," was the reply from Mrs Mitchell who had, by now, managed to gain the crest of the slope.

"I still can't see it," was my reply as I was getting more concerned that both myself and Hector weren't going to make it to the graveside!

"It is under the corrugated sheet," was the answer, and with a considerable amount of relief I spotted a corrugated sheet in the dim light. I headed towards it as quickly as I could and with a superhuman effort just managed to kick the sheet off the grave. *Phew! Thank goodness that I have just made it!* was my thought, because by now Hector was slipping from my arms and there was absolutely no possibility of me holding him anymore. That was when I noticed it! The grave was only about three inches deep! "Oh no! Not again!" flashed through my mind. "It's not very deep!"

Hector gently slipped from my weary arms just as Mrs Mitchell caught up with me.

"Oh. No! Hector's grave is full of water!" she exclaimed in a very distressed voice.

Hector was on his way at this point as I replied, "No! It's OK. It's just a little bit of water in the bottom of the grave." At that very second, he hit the water with a splash!

I was completely wrong of course because it had been raining heavily all day and the 'run off' water had drained into the grave, which was actually about 5-feet-deep! My erroneous comment of being 'just a little bit in the bottom' was soon proven to be 'gravely' mistaken as Hector disappeared out of sight! Glug, glug and he was gone, only to reappear a moment or two later and then he continued to bob up and down, up and down in the water!

Thoroughly soaked, exhausted and miserable by this point I could do no more than make a rapid exit and to leave the final funeral arrangements to the gardener on the next day! I was convinced that Mrs Mitchell expected me to exhume or fish Hector out of his watery grave! I did, however, replace the cover on the grave and headed for home, soaked and shattered! Once more saying to myself, "Never, ever again!"

End of life situations are really most important to pet owners and we always endeavoured to make them as stress free as possible and to acquiesce to clients' wishes as far as reasonably possible, which in many cases meant visiting the client's home. Unfortunately, animals don't always pick convenient times to decide on their exit from this life and so late evening and weekend events were not uncommon.

Another busy Saturday morning clinic had just been completed and I was looking forward to getting home and spending a little time in my garden, seeing as it was an unusually warm summer's day!

"Dr Hayworth has just phoned. She was wondering if you could go and see Honey. She thinks that her time has come, and she would be very grateful if you could go and put her to sleep this afternoon?" said the receptionist as she made her exit into the sunshine.

Dr Hayworth and her husband, who was also a medic, had been really nice clients for a number of years and their Golden Retriever, Honey, I had known since she was about 8 years of age. I checked their address on the computer and saw how old Honey was. My goodness, she was 18 years of age! Quite an amazing age for her breed!

So, off I went to their house hoping that it wouldn't be too long until I was home myself. I arrived at Dr Hayworth's home to be greeted by her husband.

"Oh, thank you so much for coming. I know it's a Saturday but I don't think that we can keep Honey going any longer. We maybe should have made the decision a few days ago when her legs were getting weak, but today she can't stand up at all. My wife is pretty upset because as you know, we have no children and Honey is our family. She is sitting on the rear lawn with her just now. Would you mind just giving Honey the injection there so that we don't have to move her?"

I could tell that he was trying to be brave himself and he led me around the side of his large home to the back garden. His wife was sitting on a travelling rug stroking Honey, who I could tell had lost a considerable amount of weight since I had last attended to her.

Honey lay quietly being stroked by her owners who in turn were comforting each other. She never stirred as I clipped some fur off her front leg and then gently administered her final injection. As anticipated, she just slipped quietly away and lay peacefully on the rug.

"I will just give you a few minutes with her," I said, "I'm going back to my car and then I will come back and we can discuss what you wish to do with Honey." Off I went to my car to put my case away and I took my time clearing a space for her body, since most people wished me to take their pets away for cremation. It also gave the Hayworths a little extra private time with their 'baby'.

When I returned to the rear garden, they had both composed themselves but were obviously still quite upset.

"Would you like me to take her away now for a private cremation?" I asked.

"Well, we were actually going to ask you if you would be so kind as to bury her for us?" asked Dr Hayworth's husband.

I'm not quite sure what expression momentarily crossed my face, but he obviously saw it and quickly added, "Oh. Is alright! I have dug her grave already, I just hoped that you would be kind enough to carry her round to it and bury her for us?"

"That would be no problem at all!" I quickly said as I inwardly sighed with relief! Phew, no digging on a hot day! In an instant, all my previous large-dog interments flashed through my mind and I thought that at least this one was going to be easy!

Honey was so old and had lost so much weight that she was only about half her previous weight. Lifting her was going to be easy and there was certainly no comparison with that of lifting an obese 50kg Doberman. Honey couldn't have weighed more than 16 kgs!

I gently gathered up Honey in my arms and followed Dr Hayworth.

"I hope you don't mind doing this?" he asked me. "We are very grateful to you. I couldn't face carrying her now that she has gone. I've dug her grave in the front garden, I hope you are OK carrying her round there?"

"It's not a problem," I replied, just being extremely relieved that I wasn't going to have to dig another canine grave!

"You might feel that this a bit strange," he continued, "but when I saw her lying asleep in the sun, last weekend, in her favourite spot, she just looked so happy and relaxed. I knew that she didn't have much time left so I decided to bury her there when her time finally came, and so I just marked around her with a spade and then I dug her grave there this morning. Unfortunately, she was sleeping on my favourite flowers in the rockery but never mind I intend re-planting them on her grave."

As we rounded the corner of the house he pointed to the rockery where the grave was. Although he was a very respected, eminent consultant doctor, it was quite obvious that he had maybe missed his calling for the grave was about 5-feet-deep, had absolutely vertical sides and there was a neat mound of soil next to it on a tarpaulin. He should have been a gravedigger! It was perfect, but there was only one problem because he had literally dug around Honey and this grave was perfectly fashioned in the shape of a sleeping dog!

In normal circumstances, I would have admired his handiwork but I now had a significant dilemma on my hands. How could I possibly lower Honey, who was no longer lying in a sleeping-dog shape, with dignity, into a five-foot-deep grave with vertical sides and which bore no resemblance to her current outline! I couldn't just drop her into the abyss, nor did I have undertakers' straps with which to lower her down.

There seemed to be only one solution in order to give her a dignified burial, especially since her grieving owner was present. That was for me to jump in the grave myself and then gently lower her down, wrapped in her blanket.

That is exactly what I did but although I was able to jump down, I was up to my shoulders in the grave and then had to carefully manipulate Honey into this weirdly dog-shaped 'final resting place'! It was more easily said than done because Honey, wrapped in a blanket, was somewhat wider than the grave mouth in places and I had also to contend with manoeuvring her past my own body which was filling a large part of the excavation! However, with a little bit of perseverance and significant effort, I managed to lower Honey's body past mine! Job done! At least, that's what I thought!

Compared with my previous burials, this one was relatively easy, well that is what I thought until I realised that Honey was now resting on top of my feet, and I couldn't get out of the grave without standing on her! Oh no! Fortunately, Dr Hayworth was still watching and so with a little bit of help from him and a big effort from me, I conformed my body to 'dog shaped' and he pulled me out from what seemed like the depths of the earth!

Thus, without wrecking my back or getting soaking wet this time the end result of my burial was just needing to get soil brushed off me!

Definitely, no more burials for me! I had never aspired to being an undertaker and fortunately, that, in fact was my last one!

Well, almost! Despite my best efforts to avoid burials, I was called to euthanize an old family horse who had reached the end of her days. This was no problem apart from the fact of the owners deciding to bury her in their own field at the side of their house. They had dug a massive grave with a JCB. Brilliant, I thought this should be easy! All I need to do is quietly euthanize their old horse and I knew that would be quick, painless and efficient. I would soon be finished and onto my next call.

However, I then got the most unusual request ever. "Could you put her to sleep next to the grave so that when she has gone, she falls into the grave. We have put her blanket in the grave and she can be buried on it. We can't face dragging her over to it when she's gone. She was very special to us all."

We led Beauty over to the grave; the family said their final farewells and I put her to sleep and with what I thought was great deal of skill I managed to get her to roll into the grave after she had gently laid down on the ground. That was the only part that I had control of because there was no way that I could control the way that she landed. Rearranging her 450kg body into some sort of peaceful repose, which was by now an upside-down body, some ten feet down in the earth was, I'm afraid, out of the question and I had to leave her somewhat unhappy owners to either fill in the grave or reposition her themselves. My life as an undertaker was definitely over now!

Unusual Encounters

"Your surgery has just phoned. Could you give them a ring when you're finished with the cows, please?" asked Morag as she came into the byre. "They have another call for you. I think they said it was a camel, but I'm not sure if I heard correctly!" she added. "Morag was a lovely, honest person who took life very seriously and I really couldn't imagine her pulling my leg!"

"A camel!" I responded with a rather incredulous look. "Aye, that will be right! April fool!" because it was the morning of 1 April! Morag looked a bit shocked at the suggestion that I thought that she would even consider telling me anything but the truth! I asked her if I could use her phone to check in with the surgery.

"I gather there is a call to see a camel?" I enquired, admittedly in a rather sceptical manner! "Where exactly is this camel supposed to be?"

"It's in Blackbridge," came the reply.

"Blackbridge?" I scoffed. "A camel in Blackbridge! Now you are having me on! Exactly whereabouts is it supposed to be then?"

"It's behind the police station, apparently," replied the receptionist.

"You do know that it is 1 April, don't you?" I asked her, "I'm sure that it is a 'wind up' and somebody is having us on!"

"I don't think so," she answered. "They sounded really genuine and worried, and they asked for you personally."

So, I got in my car and headed off to Blackbridge, knowing that there was nowhere behind the police station and being absolutely certain that nobody in this part of the world kept camels anyway!

As I drove through the small village, I was keeping a sharp look out for some friend or other who was ready to have a laugh at my expense. I couldn't really see anybody lurking about and so I turned in towards the police station where I saw a small lane that went over the brow of the hill just behind the station. I must admit that I had never noticed it before but on the other hand I usually did my best to avoid police stations! I, somewhat gingerly, drove down the lane and crested the brow of the small hill to find a playing field that I didn't even know existed. There was no sign of anybody waiting to laugh at me either!

However, at the far end of the playing field was a tent, in fact, a rather large tent with assorted vehicles parked next to it. It was a small circus that had arrived in town! Maybe there was a camel here right enough! I felt slightly guilty that I had disbelieved the honest, sincere Morag!

I parked my car on the grass and walked over to the tent and stuck my head through the door flaps, where a rotund, florid faced man greeted me. It wasn't actually so much of a greeting as a rude inquisition!

"You the vet?" he asked rather curtly. "Know anything about camels? Treated them before?"

"Well, no, I've not treated any before," I replied and laughed, "With our rainfall, there aren't too many deserts in this part of the world!"

"Don't be funny with me," he replied. "She's sick and I need somebody who knows what they are doing to fix her!"

"Well, what seems to be the trouble?" I asked him, suitably chastened. This guy was a pretty crusty sort of character but, in fairness, he was probably fairly worried about his sick camel.

"She's got a wire stuck down her throat," was his brusque reply. "I can't get it out meself like, but I will give you a torch and a step ladder and I will hold her mouth open while you put your hand down her throat and get the wire out. I'm really worried about her because she can't eat and she's in real pain."

I've got to admit that the last thing that I fancied doing was putting my arm down a camel's throat, especially whilst balanced on a stepladder and relying on an unknown person to hold her mouth open!

"What in all the world makes you think that she has a wire stuck down her throat then?" I asked him. "Have you seen her eating some wire?"

"Listen, laddie, I knows me camels and I just know that she has a wire down her throat," he retorted. "Come on, just get her fixed, like I asked!"

I wasn't too pleased by his overbearing attitude, but I didn't want to take his word for what was going on either.

"Let me examine her first and I'll see what is going on," I told him.

"I've just telt you what is wrong with her!" was the aggressive reply.

"I'm just going to the car to get my stethoscope and thermometer. Where is she anyway?"

He just shook his head in disbelief. "You don't need them. It's a wire! Do you hear me? It's a wire! She's in the small tent. Hurry up, would you? She's getting worse by the minute!"

As I entered the tent, I could hear the camel before I even could see her because she was making the most awful bellowing, groaning sounds and trying to vomit foul smelling liquid! I appreciated his concern though because she was looking distinctly unwell and was extremely distressed.

It is always quite difficult trying to thoroughly examine a large animal when it is lying down and after checking her temperature, I asked the circus owner if he could get her to stand up for me so that I could listen to her chest and stomach.

Reluctantly he kneed the camel in her flank and at the same time shouted at her to stand up, which she slowly did. I wished that I had never asked him to get her to stand because now I could barely reach her head and mouth to examine them! Perhaps it would have been better to leave her lying down! First camel examination lesson learned!

"She's getting worse by the minute! Come on I've got the steps here, let's just get this bloody wire out!"

"She hasn't got a wire down her throat," I announced rather bravely. "She's got rhododendron poisoning."

"What?" he bellowed. "Don't be stupid! How could you possibly think that? Just my luck to get a vet that knows nothing about camels. She's really valuable you know?"

I might not have treated camels before, but I had seen and treated sheep and goats with rhododendron poisoning in the past and I certainly wasn't letting that on to him!

"Let's hope that she hasn't eaten too much because there is no specific antidote to the poison, but I will give her some injections and we will dose her with medicine over her throat. Just need to keep our fingers crossed that she responds quickly."

"Rhododendron poisoning indeed! Never heard the likes of it! How could she possibly get that?" was his acerbic reply but which was quickly followed by, "Eh. My goodness. Damnation! You might be right. We were down by a river last night in a country estate and I let them free for a bit of exercise and a drink and they were surrounded by rhododendrons! Do you think she ate some?"

"Absolutely positive," I replied, as I breathed an inward sight of relief!

I had never injected a camel before, and I needed to give her an injection into the jugular vein in her neck. "What is she going to do when I inject her? How will she react?" I enquired.

"Nothing," was the short answer. "I will tie her head to this rail at the front of her stall and you can inject her."

That was exactly what he did, and the treatment was given without incident and without any resistance from the camel. I left the owner with his camel and went away to complete my morning round of visits, musing to myself about how life was never dull and boring, and I hadn't been April fooled either!

"Call me if she's worse or not improving by this afternoon," was my final instruction.

There was no further word that day from the circus about the camel and so the next morning, when I was passing, I nipped in to see whether she had improved or maybe just to see if she had even survived! There was nobody about and so

I walked into the tent to see the camel. To my huge relief, it was standing up eating, was looking quite alert and more importantly had stopped groaning and vomiting! I thought that I would just give her a quick check over and I walked over to her, lifted her tail to check her temperature, only to be forcibly knocked out of the way by a blow to my shoulders from behind me!

"What in all the world do you think you are doing?" was the question from an incredulous circus owner. "She'll have you! She's a bad un you know?"

"You didn't say that yesterday!" was my flustered reply.

"Nay laddie, didn't need to. She was sick yesterday!"

"Thankfully, she does seem to be a lot better today though." I observed and since the man seemed to be of a better disposition, I asked him why he had phoned for me, in particular, to see his camel.

"I didn't!" was the short answer. "I phoned a safari park to see if I could get hold of their vet because I knew that they had camels. When I eventually spoke to him, and he asked me what was wrong with the camel I told him about the wire being stuck down her throat and how I had the step ladder and the torch ready and as quick as a flash he gave me your number and said the local vet could deal with that!"

"Ha, ha! There's nothing like passing the buck!" I said. "But all is well that ends well! I am so glad that she is OK now though."

"So am I! I thought we'd lost her yesterday! You got kiddies? Here's three tickets for the matinee tomorrow."

That gesture was certainly unexpected but was most kind. I was just elated that the camel had recovered and just as importantly that I had been correct with my diagnosis!

'Expect the unexpected' would be a suitable maxim for general mixed practice. Knowing exactly **what** to expect, however is a completely different thing.

"Could you get to Kilburn, please, there is someone who has just been on the phone with a lame zebra?" asked the receptionist.

"You're joking, are you absolutely certain?" I questioned her, "Or are you just pulling my leg?" I really couldn't envisage the existence of a piece of the African plains in that part of the world, nor was there, to the best of my knowledge a Zoo.

"Ha, ha, no! It's no joke, he was calling from a circus apparently. Have fun!"

I had never had a zebra as a patient before but as I drove along the road, I surmised that it was really only a stripy kind of horse, which I was certainly familiar with, and it might even be well trained, and certainly easy to handle. As I located the 'big top', which wasn't really that big, I was wondering what tricks the zebra might perform in the circus and what other animals they might have there too.

"Are you the vet? Thank you for coming. One of the zebras is lame and we can't put him in the ring the way that he is. He's over there in that pen," as the circus owner waved his hand in the direction of a rather agitated, snorting zebra.

The zebra certainly looked lame and was not fully weight bearing on his left foreleg which was swollen just above the hoof. I thought that he probably had an infection in his foot, and I would need to examine him further and explore the sole of his foot with my hoof knife.

"It looks like a hoof abscess," I said. "Can you catch him for me so that I can lift his foot and examine it?"

"Er, well, no!" was the answer. "I can't catch him but he will take bread from me! I'll go and get a loaf from the caravan," and with that he disappeared and left me contemplating the distinctly unfriendly patient. Maybe the zebra didn't understand my version of Swahili because he certainly didn't respond to my 'soothing' talk!

The circus owner arrived back fairly quickly and started to throw slices of white bread to the zebra, which, with great skill, caught them in his mouth. We both climbed over the fence into the pen and as he fed the Zebra more slices of bread, I approached his shoulder area and attempted to lift his foot. That was a bad mistake, as I quickly found out, since this zebra could leap in the air and kick with all four feet simultaneously whilst both eating bread and trying to bite my arm off! A talented performer indeed! Having got so roused up, the pen wasn't exactly a safe place to stay in and we both leaped over the pen as with ears back and teeth bared this demonic animal chased us out!

It was becoming quite obvious that if I was going to examine the foot properly then I would need to sedate the Zebra. How were we going to catch him though was the question? I had no access to a dart gun or pole syringe to inject him with sedative and his owner couldn't catch him so I resorted to what I had done in the past when I couldn't catch intractable cows or horses. I returned to my car for my lasso! A few years previously I had been shown how to lasso animals by an old 'cowboy' who had retired from Calgary to his home country of Scotland. His proficiency with a lasso was absolutely amazing and although I would never reach his level of skill, I practiced like mad and soon was passably able at catching things, including my poor old dog who was often used as a practice subject! The poor old soul got to the stage where he wouldn't run in front of me without looking over his shoulder for the approaching rope! Lassoing was a great skill to have if there were animals to be caught and where there was insufficient help to do so. It certainly had saved me a lot of wasted time and frustration in the past.

I returned with my treasured lasso, confident that the problem with the zebra would soon be satisfactorily resolved, for I had never been defeated with an animal…yet!

With a deft flick of my arm and wrist, I caught the zebra with my first throw and quickly looked around for somewhere to anchor the rope to, so that I could 'reel' him in and restrain him for administering a sedative. I rapidly wrapped the rope around a stout pole and began reeling the zebra in towards me, a procedure which only increased his anger and rage! Just as I almost had him pulled up against the edge of his pen and while he was leaping up and down, kicking and screaming like a thing possessed, he suddenly broke free! My lasso had snapped! I was dumbfounded for it had never happened before and as I turned round to the circus owner, I saw him standing there with a huge knife in his hand and the remains of the rope. He had cut my precious lasso!

"What in all the world did you do that for?" I asked him rather angrily.

"Because you tied him to the central pole of the big top and he was going to bring the whole bloody thing crashing down! Can you not just give me some medicine for him, and we will see how he gets on?"

I had never been defeated before, nor since, in my attempts to examine an animal but his suggestion seemed like a reasonable option in the situation. So, with the aid of a few loaves of bread, the zebra was going to get a course of powdered medication.

"That animal is totally mad and wild," I observed. "What exactly is he trained to do in the circus?"

"Oh, he's not trained," was the reply. "See that other zebra over there? Well, she is trained to run round the ring and jump through hoops of fire and over obstacles etc. This one, he's not trained at all. He just follows the other one around the ring. We've just borrowed him from a Safari Park down south for the summer. He's completely wild! He eats bread from us but we can't really get near him."

"Well, that's just fantastic! Thanks for telling me now!"

That certainly explained a lot! My precious lasso ruined too!

Only a few days later I had another interesting and potentially traumatic visit. A local doctor who seemed more interested in his menagerie of exotic animals than his patients asked me to castrate his stroppy, male, somewhat aggressive llama!

"Come up and see him, could you? I need to discuss his behaviour with you. He'd becoming quite dominant and aggressive, and I suspect it's because he's sexually mature now and his hormones are bothering him!"

I duly arrived at his small farm where he showed me his various pets and then introduced me to his llama.

"Don't stand too close to the pen because he will either spit at you or bite you if you are close enough! I am the only person that can handle him but, to be quite honest, I'm beginning to find him quite a handful and I suspect that it is only a matter of time before he seriously harms me! Do you think that I should get him castrated? I really can't see any other option."

I agreed with his assessment of the situation and then he asked, "Have you ever castrated a llama before?"

I had to admit that I had castrated literally hundreds of animals of different types but that I had never castrated a llama.

"I hope you don't mind, but I've photocopied a page out of a 'Llama' book, and I have highlighted a passage in it that maybe you would care to read before you do the deed. I think that it may be of interest to you!"

We arranged a date and time to carry out the surgery and I left with the document. The photocopy described fighting and aggression in male llamas and how they would face each other when they were fighting, striking out with their front legs and then, with sweeping head and neck movements would try and bite or even remove their opponent's genitals. The part that he had highlighted read 'and they will try and do the same to human males too!'

A man with a wry sense of humour! I'm pleased to report that the whole procedure went smoothly and without untoward happenings and both the human males retained, without injury, their respective reproductive organs!

Equine Encounters

It was Saturday lunch time and having just finished a busy consulting hour, I was hoping for a quiet afternoon and maybe even being able to get some lunch before the weekend 'on call' emergencies started. As I packed my instruments away and prepared to leave, the receptionist came into the consulting room and told me that I had a call to go and see a lame horse.

"Oh! Just fantastic!" I muttered to myself. "Why this afternoon? Was it urgent or extremely lame?" I asked her.

"They were a bit vague; they've only had it for about a week and they are very worried about it. It is their daughter's first pony apparently and it's at Rannoch Farm."

"Oh well, at least it is in the general direction of my home. I'd better get off and see it then. Goodbye."

"I hope that you have a quiet weekend. Goodbye and good luck," she replied as I left.

Hmm. I vaguely wondered why she added 'good luck' and set off in my car.

I arrived at the stables and then I wandered around looking for somebody with a lame horse. Eventually, I found a young girl who was busily talking to and stroking a rather stout pony. She must only have been about 9 or 10 years of age.

"I'm looking for someone with a lame pony. Have you seen anyone else about?" I asked her.

"No. There's no one else here. Are you the vet? It is my new pony that is lame. My mum phoned for you." She replied in a rather timid manner.

"Where is your mum then?" I asked her because ethically, and sensibly, animals shouldn't be treated unless there was a person of adult age present.

"Oh! Mum and Dad are away shopping for the afternoon. They said just to send your bill once you've sorted my pony."

"Away shopping? I really shouldn't be looking at the pony unless they are here. Can you get in touch with them?"

"No. They said I was just to stay here until they got back."

Oh! Just wonderful I thought to myself. I couldn't guarantee to come back later since I was on call and various other emergencies would probably need seeing.

The little girl was dressed in the best of 'gear'. Jodhpurs, gilet, boots and the regulation baseball cap which seemed to be the required uniform for young horse-owning girls!

"Are you able to hold the pony while I look at him? What is his name?"

"Oh yes! I can hold him OK," she replied, "and his name is Bramble."

Brambled eyed me somewhat suspiciously as I entered the stable.

"Right! You just hold him there and I will pick out his feet. How long have you had Bramble for then?" I asked as I approached him and petted his neck. "Where did you get him from?" I asked by way of conversation.

"I'm not sure," she said, "My dad got him from a yard somewhere that sold lots of horses."

"So how long has he been lame for?"

"Well, he's not so much lame as he's got sore feet." She added.

"I see," I said, "I had better have a look at them then." Fat ponies like Bramble quite commonly had laminitis when they were 'sore' on their feet and often had a characteristic stance, which Bramble wasn't showing any evidence of.

I struggled to lift his fore feet and to clean the soles with my hoof knife. Bramble wasn't the most co-operative of patients and in addition, as I bent over, he tried to bite lumps out of my backside! A dainty, young girl was no match for holding a wilful, strong pony! There appeared to be no pain nor heat in the hooves, and he didn't react adversely to my using my 'hoof testers' to see whether his hooves had any pain in them.

Picking up his front feet was bad enough but trying to pick up his back feet was a completely different kettle of fish! Bramble just went absolutely crazy! No sooner had I started to touch his lower back leg than he erupted! He kicked out wildly then bucked with both hind legs in the air, hitting the stable wall with some force. After getting battered and bruised by this wild creature, I thought I would try and lift his opposite hind leg, since I had totally failed with the nearside one! This was an even worse idea and not only was I getting bashed and squashed against the wall, I was concerned that the little girl was going to get injured, since Bramble was now pirouetting around the stable and dragging her about with him, having the odd kick at me when he got a chance! I had no intention of being defeated by Bramble, but I was also getting fed up getting bruised and kicked.

"OK," I panted. "Let's take him outside and trot him up and down and see if I can see why he's lame."

Bramble obviously thought this was a great idea and he rushed past us into the stable passage, dragging the young girl with him! To her credit, she held on valiantly and trotted the pony up and down for me. He wasn't showing any signs of lameness!

"He's not lame," I announced. "Why did you think he was lame?"

"Well, it is just that we've never been able to lift his back feet up. So, we thought that there must be something wrong with them. They must be sore! My dad got the farrier to come out during the week and he couldn't lift them either and my dad got kicked too! So, the farrier said to call the vet."

"Just tell your dad to phone me when he gets home then. Bramble isn't lame nor sore. I wonder if anybody has ever managed to lift his feet up easily. There's no medicine that is going to fix that!"

Bramble had been sold by an unscrupulous dealer as a suitable 'first pony' to people who had plenty money but who had no equine experience. It was quite obvious that Dad didn't intend getting kicked again either. Even Saturday afternoon shopping with his wife was a better option! Bramble was soon returned to the dealer, however!

Horses are often afflicted with colic, an extremely painful and potentially even fatal condition unless it is treated promptly. The horses will sometime violently roll or throw themselves about in an effort to get away from or relieve the severe abdominal discomfort that they are experiencing. Some may advance to a torsion of their intestinal tract in which case they will certainly die unless they have a successful surgical procedure! Every case of colic is most concerning until it is resolved.

Many cases seem to happen at night and I was forever getting called out to one particular stables, owned by a relatively new client who owned a small livery stable and who was reasonably pleasant and apparently grateful enough that his horses were seen promptly, but who on the other hand, never paid his bills!

Reminder after reminder was sent to him about paying his account and every time that he was about to be told to get veterinary attention elsewhere, he would phone up once more with a horse with colic! We are under an obligation to see animals that are in distress and so I was obliged to attend to these cases, usually after midnight, and always urgently. I couldn't refuse to go! Equally, in the middle of the night and when his horse was recovering. He would faithfully promise to settle his bill.

He was informed that we just couldn't keep coming out if he didn't pay! Of course, payment never materialised and before we could send his account to the debt collectors, he would phone up once again with a horse in distress with colic! I never, ever attended during daylight hours. It was always at night.

Enough was enough, he had a relatively large account outstanding. I finally decided to get our lawyers to sue him and also to inform him that we weren't going to provide any more veterinary attention for his animals. He would need to register with another veterinary practice.

Almost immediately, I got a surprise telephone call from our lawyers.

"Do you realise who it is that you have asked us to pursue through the courts?"

"Why, yes, of course, he's Mr O'Shea with that large account which has been outstanding for ages."

I duly recounted the story about all the evening/night call outs and how every time we resolved not to go back to his place he would phone up with another emergency!

"If you have any sense at all, you will just drop it. Just write it off," was the legal eagle's response!

"No way!" I replied. "I have spent so many nights at that place over the last few months. It's always after midnight too. I have had enough of him just using us."

"If you've any sense, you will drop it! Just put it down to a bad experience! We are definitely **not** pursuing him for you," quickly adding, "There's not a lawyer in the whole of Scotland that will do that for you! Do you know that if you persist, he will come and break your arms and legs, or do even worse things! He would do the same to us! He's a high-end criminal you know. One of the worst in the country! Just leave it be and continue to live!"

I must admit that I was absolutely incensed and was not inclined to take the lawyer's advice, but I was persuaded to heed it when he said that even my family could be put at risk. O'Shea obviously lived by intimidation, threats and instilling fear into people, and it didn't sit well with me!

A short time later, on a snowy afternoon, I got a call to attend a local police station. As is usual, I didn't get many details about why I was to attend until I got there! When I arrived, I was told that it was a rather unusual case involving a horse.

Apparently, there was a dispute concerning an unpaid livery bill for a pony. The owner of the pony had for some reason refused to pay his livery bill and he had then received his horse's ears through the post! The police officer told me where the livery stables were, and it was a place that I didn't recognise the name of. The question that the police were asking was whether the pony was alive or dead when its ears were cut off! Apparently, the body was now lying in a field, in the snow, minus its ears!

"OK then. Let's go," I said, "It will be dark soon."

"Oh! We can't go yet!" said the Officer. "We'll need to wait for others. This guy is a real problem character and he will play off one of us against the other, report us to the Chief constable, no matter how civil we are and no matter how much we follow the correct procedures, he will report us. In addition, it is well known that he can be pretty violent!"

Another officer appeared and I said, "Let's go then."

"Oh. We can't go yet! There are not enough of us! We need at least three officers to be on the safe side."

So, we duly had to wait for the arrival of a third police officer before we set out. None of them looked too happy about visiting this guy. I suppose getting horse's ears through the post had a semblance of a mafia type person! If postage wasn't so expensive it sounded as though he would probably have sent the whole head!

"You come with us in our vehicles," I was instructed.

"It's OK, I will come behind you in my own car because I have everything in it that I might need."

I followed the police vehicles and we arrived at a field. "The pony is across in that bog. You can see it partially submerged. Oh! Here he comes now! You stick in the middle

125

between the three of us and you should be fairly safe. We will try and protect you," and in unison their hands all gripped the handles of their truncheons.

The livery owner got nearer and I suddenly recognised him as the notorious Mr O'Shea! Well, well, well!

"I know him!" I said to the police officers, "I just didn't know he had this livery yard too."

"Oh, it's yourself!" Mr O'Shea said to me. Not appearing in the least bit violent but not having much to say to the police officers either.

We traversed the field in silence, and I waded into the bog to examine the earless pony, which looked as though it had been dead for some time. There was no sign of any bleeding from the head wounds and it did, indeed, appear as though the ears had been removed after death rather than from it when it was alive. A proper and full post-mortem was really needed and because it was now dark and the pony needed to be extricated from the bog this was not going to be carried out that night.

As a professional witness, one has to make an impartial report on the facts of a case, and one shouldn't be making any comments about it to an alleged perpetrator.

"It was an old pony, decrepit old thing. It was on its last legs. Obviously got stuck in the bog and died," he informed me.

"That doesn't really explain why it doesn't appear to have any ears though!" I replied.

"Oh, that's them foxes. They're hungry at this time of year and they will chow anything," was his answer. "They allus start with the ears. Them's soft and tasty-like," said with no trace of embarrassment or shame. He obviously thought that

I was gullible enough to 'swallow' his explanation. I was so tempted, but obviously couldn't, ask him exactly which post office these foxes had used to post the ears!

"I will get the pony removed tomorrow and will get a full post-mortem examination done," I told him.

"Please yourself," was his uncaring response.

As is often the case, prosecutions can take forever to reach the courts and this one was no exception! However, most unusually, it was dropped!

That certainly was a little bit puzzling, because it was a horrible case, but it turned out that the case was dropped because the man in question, Mr O'Shea, had been in court for a much more serious case. He was now residing 'at Her Majesty's pleasure' in prison. Somebody had 'crossed him' and he was now doing time for their murder!

Maybe, just sometimes, it is worth heeding your lawyer's advice!

"This is Paddy Reilly here. Would you be as good as to come and check my horse for me? To be sure now, I know it is late at night, but she's right bad with the colic and although I haven't used you before, I've heard you're mighty good with these cases. She's a top class show jumper and really valuable and I'd be truly obliged if you'd come as soon as you can. She's 'trowing' herself about the stable now as we speak!"

Paddy was full of the blarney and although I wasn't taken in by his silvery tongue I was certainly concerned for his horse. Should I refuse to go and tell him to call out his usual vet? Should I just fulfil my obligations and go? The latter being exactly what I did, of course, even though it was 12:30 a.m. and I was extremely tired.

Paddy gave me his address and instructions about how to find his place because he lived in a large house which was not visible from the main road. His directions were very good and I arrived at his house a short time later. I had to park my car and wend my way past his Range Rover, his wife's BMW and the biggest, most smart, silver and blue, horse box that one could ever imagine! It wouldn't have looked out of place at Ascot!

There was an outside light on, illuminating a row of stables and Paddy appeared from one of these loose boxes.

"Quick, quick. She's in here," he barked at me. "She's down and rolling about and sweating like the devil. She's our best horse, you know, a champion show jumper. Oh, sure now, she can jump right out of her skin can this one! Begorrah and Bejasus I am really worried about her."

I was quickly ushered into the stable to observe this large sweating horse rolling about on the floor. Examining her wasn't exactly very easy, but we managed to get her back on her feet, treated her for spasmodic colic and I waited until she had settled down and was comfortable. She passed loads of wind and then proceeded to look for hay to eat.

I gave him instructions for her aftercare and left for home relieved that she had improved and was comfortable again. He was to phone me if there were any further problems.

"Tanks very much. Molly, here, looks a lot better. She's competing again at the Horse of the Year Show again and will surely win it if she's on form. She was in fine fettle before this here bout of the colic."

Molly must have got over her colic OK for I never heard from Paddy for a few weeks until I got another early morning request to attend to another of his horses that had colic.

This happened a number of times and I began to wonder if Paddy was another 'Mr O'Shea' who always called me out at night but who never paid his bills! I did mention the outstanding account to him once or twice and how I couldn't keep going out to see his horses if he didn't pay. There were always reassurances and promises that he would do so. As with Mr O'Shea, I resolved never to go back unless there was some payment forthcoming, and as before, there was always an emergency visit needed! There seemed to be no obvious shortage of money and it was difficult to understand his lack of payment, more so since he had received excellent service and all his horses had recovered without mishap.

Then, one day, out of the blue, he telephoned the practice requesting a visit to vaccinate his horses! A during the daytime visit too for a change!

The receptionist reminded home about his outstanding account and booked the visit.

Paddy was even more jocular and affable than he usually was, and I vaccinated all his horses without incident. They were exceptionally big, attractive animals.

Just as I was getting my boots washed and disinfected, Paddy suddenly said, "You must come into the house and get your hands washed and I will settle up your account! Sure now, I know I have been a bit remiss about paying it and that it been outstanding for a while but I will get it sorted today. Good work always deserves to be rewarded."

Somewhat taken aback by his sudden desire to settle his account, I followed him into the kitchen and as I washed my hands, he rummaged through a drawer for his chequebook. As I dried my hands, I was thinking to myself about how pleased my boss would be to finally see the colour of Paddy's money!

"I know that I owe you quite a bit of money," Paddy said, "but you know, I chust can't put me hands on your bill at this moment."

After he had flattened his chequebook and smoothed down the pages, he produced an expensive looking fountain pen and with a dramatic flourish he began to write the cheque.

"Now who does I mek it out to?" he asked, followed by, "Do you remember how much it was for?"

I didn't know for certain how much his account now totalled and was just trying to remember when he said, "Sure now. I tink it was about eight hunner and fifty pounds. I'll tell you what I'll do. Seeing as you have waited so long for it I will just round it up to nine hunner," and with that he wrote in the amount and signed the cheque with a flourish.

My boss was absolutely elated when I returned waving the cheque in the air. "Paddy Reilly has just paid me! He has even had the decency to round it up for you seeing as you've waited so long for the money!"

"Give me it here then, quickly, so that I can get it in the bank today. Thank goodness that his account has been settled at last."

A few days later, and in retrospect probably not unexpectedly, the bank informed us that the cheque had 'bounced' and had not been honoured. Perhaps there had been some sort of mistake, I thought, because Paddy seemed to be really quite affluent!

We hadn't been taken a back for too long before the telephone rang and a Chief Inspector from the police asked to speak to me. I asked him what it was about and he wouldn't tell me, but asked whether he could come out and see me that afternoon or the following morning.

An arrangement was duly made and I faced the prospect of an interview with a senior police officer with considerable trepidation! As far as I could remember I hadn't done anything wrong that might involve the police and he was a much too high ranking an officer to be pursuing a traffic offence!

He arrived and introduced himself as head of the serious fraud squad and announced that he was investigating an extremely serious matter! I really couldn't imagine what I could have possibly done to merit being investigated by the fraud squad! I thought that I was absolutely honest and had never knowingly defrauded anyone!

He must have seen my reaction and facial expression because he said, "Relax, it is not about you but I need to ask you a few questions in private."

"We have reason to believe that you have had dealings with a Mr Paddy Reilly. Is that correct?"

"Why, yes, it is," I confirmed. "He lives in a big house near Levertown and I have treated his horses."

"And did he ever pay you?" the Chief Inspector asked.

I kind of laughed and replied, "He was the most reluctant payer ever, but he had paid us last week but that the cheque had bounced."

At this, his eyes lit up and he said that I had to tell him about the whole saga. I therefore recounted the tales of midnight call outs etc., and how we were always threatening to tell him we would no longer do his work etc., when then he would have another emergency.

"So, tell me EXACTLY what happened when he paid you."

So, I did my best to recount the sequence of events as he took copious notes. I went into the details of how he was unable to find our latest account and how he generously rounded up the figure since we had waited so long for payment.

At this point, he said, "Oh! You fool! You're no longer part of this investigation! He didn't defraud you! He offered you an amount of money and you took it! If he had paid your exact bill, knowing that the cheque wouldn't be honoured, then that is fraud! You weren't defrauded! How much was it for? I mean the cheque that he gave you?"

When I told him, he just laughed! At the moment, he has defrauded some well-known and famous people out of about three million pounds! He'd been persuading them to invest in non-existent schemes!

"It's really hard to believe that he is fraudster. A lovely house, fancy cars, expensive horses, an affable person etc., the last man that I would have thought would have been a fraudster," I said.

"He is **exactly** the sort of person who operates fraudulent schemes! A glib, smooth operating con man!" added the Inspector. "Thank you for your help. You are now excluded from our investigations and I'm sorry to say that you will never get your account settled either!"

It takes all sorts!

Your Life in Their Hands, or in Their Teeth and Claws! Narrow Escapes!

"Can you come and do a visit this afternoon please? We haven't seen our old male lynx for a couple of days, and he hasn't eaten any of his food. We'd like to you check him out if he's still alive because he might even be dead!"

As, is often the case, the afternoon call from a zoo park came in when I was very busy and when the daylight would be fading fast, being late autumn/winter time. I set off for the park, not having any idea of what I was going to encounter and at the same time relishing the prospect of dealing with something different. Lynx weren't everyday patients, but I had dealt with some before and they certainly weren't to be messed with!

I arrived at the park as the light was beginning to fade and met the manager who relayed her worries about the old lynx to me. There was apparently every chance that he might be dead, but they were unable to be absolutely certain because they couldn't see into his den! He had an inside den, which was accessible, and an outside den in his enclosure which certainly wasn't accessible but served as a safe retreat for him.

We entered the pen, which was strewn with uneaten food and searched the general area of the enclosure. There was certainly no sign of him so he must be in the outside den. The den looked very natural, being covered in grassy turf but unfortunately it had been constructed like an Eskimo's igloo with an entrance that was a tunnel of about 6-feet-long and which then led into a sleeping area. A problem! There was no access to the den apart from going down the fairly narrow tunnel.

Nobody was willing to go into the den and so it was left to me to see whether the lynx had died in the den. Armed with a torch and a brush that I had commandeered from a keeper, I had to get down on my stomach and crawl into the tunnel, holding the torch in my mouth and using the brush as a potential weapon of defence in case I met the lynx trying to attack me or to escape past me! I inched my way down the tunnel on my abdomen like a Royal Marine at a training camp. It was pitch black of course and as I got halfway down the tunnel, by the light of my torch, I saw a sudden flash of large white teeth accompanied by a throaty growl and a sharp hiss!

"He is definitely alive!" I tried to call out over my shoulder. A difficult thing to do with a torch in one's mouth! I rapidly reversed out of the lynx's igloo!

"Well, he's obviously not very well," responded the keepers, "because he would normally have had you by now! He's not very sociable!" This was probably the understatement of the year!

"So, what are you going to do now?" they asked, almost in unison. "Will we need to dig out the tunnel or dig through the concrete into his nest area? That's a big job at this time of night!"

Having pondered the situation for a few moments I decided that the only thing to do was for me to go back down the tunnel with a dog-catching pole, snare the lynx and then sedate him once I had caught him! Easy to say, but much harder to do! So off I went back to my car for some drugs and the keepers went to fetch their dog-catching pole.

At that point in my life, I had never sedated a lynx before, far less caught one and so I had to quickly estimate his weight and work out a dose of drugs to give him. I surmised that he was just really a bigger version of a pet cat, albeit with a slightly different personality, and so I mixed a combination of cat drugs, in a syringe, to administer to him! But first I needed to catch my patient!

Equipped with a dog-pole and with the torch back in my mouth I gingerly inched my way back down the tunnel. It seemed to be an even longer tunnel than last time and it was no easy feat to manoeuvre the pole and myself down it. Most fortunately the lynx hadn't moved and appeared reluctant to do so, but as I got near him with the noose on the end of the pole he suddenly erupted into a wide mouthed, spitting ball of white-toothed fury!

After numerous unsuccessful attempts to get the noose over his head because I was trying to do it single-handedly in the confines of the tunnel, I eventually managed to get the noose over his head and to tighten it as much as I dared. Then began the difficult task of reversing out of the tunnel and at the same time towing a very reluctant and objecting 35 kg lynx with me! As soon as I exited the tunnel I handed the pole, with lynx attached, to one of the keepers and then quickly injected the irate cat with the drug cocktail that I had prepared earlier. It normally can take ten to twenty minutes for sedation to take full effect but within five minutes the lynx was completely anaesthetised and immobile! What a relief, but the real question was what to do next because after a quick examination of the animal it became apparent that he would need some blood samples taken and fluid therapy administered if he was going to be given the best chance of recovery.

The only solution was to transport him back to my surgery where I could deal with him and so between us, we successfully got him into a large, wire mesh cage which was in the boot of my estate car. With a considerable sense of relief, I then sped away to my surgery, which was about 12 miles away, desperately hoping there would be no mishaps on the way and that the lynx would remain 'asleep'! I needn't have worried because the lynx was still pretty zonked out and it was no great problem lifting him from my car into the surgery.

An IV drip was quickly connected to a catheter placed in the lynx's foreleg and I quickly took some blood samples from him. The blood results were obtained, the lynx was still immobile on the operating room table, and we deduced that he was badly dehydrated, had an infection and was really just an old boy with age related problems. He was placed in a large hospital cage and then we monitored him closely. We didn't reverse his sedation but allowed him to 'come' round from it naturally. Eight hours later it was obvious that the sedation had finally worn off and we were greeted with a curled lip and a snarl!

We kept him in for a few days and it was quite obvious that as he began eating again and was obviously improving that it was becoming unsafe and unwise to keep him in a surgery environment!

I knew he would need to be sedated for his trip back to the park and that he had 'slept' for a long time after the initial sedation and therefore I decided to give him a smaller dose of sedative because I only needed to transport him about 12 miles. I didn't want him to sleep for eight hours this time!

Once he was sufficiently sedated, I bundled him into the back of my car and set off for his home. The journey was uneventful, and I sighed with relief as I turned into the tradesmen's entrance to the park which was about 200 yards long. I'd soon have him home and off my hands. A healthy lynx once more!

Those thoughts had hardly passed through my mind when I drove, maybe rather too quickly, over the first of two speed bumps and became aware of a movement from the boot area. A quick glance in the mirror and to my absolute horror, I saw a head with two tasselled ears trying to sit up in the back of my car! Oh no!

I almost took off over the next speed bump as I accelerated as fast as I could into the zoo park yard. I shouted to the keepers for help and at the same time commandeered a wheelbarrow from a passing and surprised groundsman, rapidly emptying it of the manure that it was carrying. The lynx was beginning to sway about in a somewhat drunken fashion as I opened the car boot and quickly but carefully dragged him out and into the wheelbarrow.

I suspect that he hadn't had a ride in a wheelbarrow before and he didn't seem to be particularly impressed with this mode of transport since he did his best to get out of it! We set off at Olympic-sprint speed with a keeper pushing the wheelbarrow and with me trying to keep the increasingly more active animal in it. Fortunately, it was not far to his pen, and we just made it to his enclosure as he began to clamber out of his transport. There, we quickly and unceremoniously dumped him into his pen and slammed the gate shut!

It was quite obvious what had happened! I had given him a lesser dose of sedative for his return journey because I didn't want him to stay sedated for eight hours, like he had done on the first occasion. However, what I hadn't really taken into account was the fact that he was ill and dehydrated the first time but was now relatively well and so the smaller dose wore off much more quickly!

Sometime later I had occasion to be back at the park and for an unknown reason was idly examining their dogcatcher which was constructed with a braided wire-filament cord covered with a plastic sheath. To my great astonishment, this dogcatcher had only one wire of this multi-filament cord that was intact and all that had been restraining the lynx as I pulled him out of his den was a plastic coating and one single strand of wire! A close call indeed!

'Close-calls' can happen to any vet in large animal practice and being chased or kicked by irate cows and bulls or by wild, uncontrolled horses are not uncommon experiences. Some events, however, end up being much more dangerous than others! Perhaps 'expect the unexpected' would be a good motto!

"Our European Bison is not very well. He's sitting in the middle of his field and won't get up. Can you come and see him please?" For those who aren't familiar with this particular type of bison, they are much taller and larger than their American cousins which are seen in countless 'Cowboy

Westerns' and are, in my experience anyway, much more irritable and temperamental. I arrived at the park soon after the phone call and met the very capable and cheerful head keeper, Philip.

"Well, Philip, what do you think is wrong with the bison today?"

"He's just not himself. He hasn't been up on his feet for 24 hours and he seems to be scouring (diarrhoea). Shall we go and have a look at him?"

The bison was sitting in the middle of his paddock looking extremely miserable with his head on the ground. "That's just how he has been. He never even got up for his feed this morning."

We both looked at the animal, who, certainly didn't look very well and discussed what we should do.

There was no easy solution to the problem. It was impossible to make a diagnosis from the distance and he was obviously quite unwell. Darting him wasn't possible since there were few licensed dart gun operators in Scotland in those days and the earliest that we could have acquired the services of one would have been the next day at the very earliest.

We elected to switch off the electric fence while we went into the field in which he was lying, open the gate and enter it. We observed him from the distance, and he never stirred or even seemed to notice us. He was lying, or at least sitting, about 100 yards away from the gate.

"Would it help if I got a sample of what he has been passing?" asked Philip and he started off, walking in a large arc so that he would eventually come round behind the bison. He was about three quarters of the way around this large arc and was starting to turn in towards where the bison was lying so that he would be approaching from its rear, when I decided to walk slowly over to where the bison was lying. It paid no attention to me and so I continued walking towards it. Then, ever so slowly it began to stand up and stretch.

Maybe it's really not too bad then, I thought to myself and at that very moment it turned towards me and started ambling slowly in my general direction.

The question in my mind was whether it was just heading for the gate, where it usually got fed, or whether it was heading towards me! That question was soon resolved because as I changed my direction, then so did the bison and it became quite apparent that it was heading straight for me! It lowered its massive head, as bison do, and kept walking in my direction.

I quickly weighed up the distance I had come from the gate and the distance that the bison now was from me and then realised that there was no way that I could retrace my steps rapidly enough to exit the field without being caught by the bison! Fortuitously, I spotted a metal girder that had been sunk into the ground in preparation for the construction of a new shelter for the animal and I sidled over to it as rapidly as I could only to watch the bison change direction too and I could now second-guess its intentions! They weren't exactly amicable ones!

I just managed to reach the post before the bison did, otherwise I don't think I would be here today, for as I reached this post which was probably about eight inches wide, so did the bison and a piece of vertical metal was all that was separating us. People say that when they are drowning, their whole life passes before their eyes in seconds and I can sort of identify with those thoughts since my own end looked as though it might be near! I remembered seeing films of cowboys and buffalos as a child and the abiding picture was of a huge furry animal with an enormous head, horns, bulging eyes and 'steam' coming out its nostrils and this was exactly what I was faced with!

The bison, who now seemed to be quite angry had its head against the post that I was standing behind and was pushing against it with all its might! I could smell his hot breath and actually touch his great big hairy head and both of its horns, with one on either side of the post. No matter in which direction I moved, this irate animal did the same as we both moved from side to side on opposite sides of the post! The bulging, angry eyes and the bellowing nostrils were not exactly giving me any reassurances that I was going to have a good chance of surviving this encounter.

We probably only dodged and swung about facing each other for a couple of minutes and I really couldn't envisage a happy resolution to this stand off! In fact, the only resolution seemed to be that I would be gored by this huge animal! I suddenly developed a huge amount of respect for the American Indians who shot these creatures with bows and arrows! It was certainly too far for me to make a run for it to the perimeter fence, and besides it was deep mud all the way there. I probably would have managed about two steps before I was tossed in the air!

The side-to-side movement and swaying about became faster and wilder and I found myself having to move really, really quickly to keep the post between me and this snorting animal. Philip, the keeper had seen what was going on and very sensibly had made a run for the opposite end of the field, which was about 300 yards away! Luckily, on one of the wilder swings around the post, the bulging, bionic eyes spied the fleeing figure heading for the far edge of the field and he set off at great speed to try and catch him! He was like a greyhound coming out of a trap and it was quite impressive, in a frightening way, how fast he could run!

I surprised myself with how fast I could run too! As soon as his back was turned, I set off running as fast as I could through the deep mud, even whilst wearing wellington boots, and crashed right through the electric fence, not caring whether it was on or off and then out of the gate. Usain Bolt could not have run any faster! Safe, but I must admit to having a slightly wobbly feeling as I stood there regaining my breath! Fortunately, Philip reached the perimeter fence before the bison and dived through the electric fence and over the barrier in record time too!

Only a few days later, this powerful, crazed animal attacked and even managed to overturn a tractor which had been driven into the field! Definitely a lucky escape for us both!

Perhaps the above was why health and safety officers were invented and why the 'fun' was taken out of life!

On another occasion when I was involved in sedating a Brown bear and moving it to a new enclosure within a zoo, the inclusion of a health and safety officer in planning the procedure, ended up with 25 people being involved and if there had been any mishaps, they would have all ended up falling over each other! We had a dart gun operator who was backed up by someone with a rifle, who was then backed up by somebody else with a shotgun, just in case the first marksman missed his target etc., etc., overkill didn't describe it! He also organised 10 men to lift the sedated bear on a stretcher where probably only six were needed because each man was only supposed to lift 20kg! These stretcher-bearers were big strapping lumberjacks too!

The one thing that he didn't take into account was that after the bear was sedated, someone (i.e., ME!) had to go into the pen and walk across wet, algae covered slippery concrete to see if the bear was properly sedated or whether he was just lying sleeping! Happily, there were no mishaps, but I must admit that it seemed like a long walk across the pen to prod the bear with a stick to test his reactions! (Or lack of them, hopefully!) My stick was about 8-feet-long but by the time I got near the bear it felt as though it had shrunk to eight inches! No mishaps, fortunately, but in future we did our own health and safety assessments!

I'm not belittling health and safety assessments, but this 'new' industry has always existed and used to be called common sense!

Car Tyre in the Rain

In the distant past, as a young graduate and as was the tradition at that time, I was issued with a practice car. In keeping with the parsimonious nature of my boss, it was, of course, the smallest car that could be purchased! It was a mini (obviously one of the original models) of the clubman or 'estate' variety. There should have been a reasonable amount of room within it for a mixed practitioner's drugs and equipment but because it was given to me with the rear seats folded down and the whole boot area occupied by an enormous wire cage, it meant that the only place to store things was underneath the front passenger seat (which could be folded over) or in the space along the edges of the cage.

Wellington boots and protective clothing could be jammed in along one side of the cage whilst the other side was filled with a metal petrol can. This petrol can was apparently the most essential item of equipment since it contained a gallon of petrol which was a reserve supply that enabled the driver to reach one particular garage from any point in the practice if one had the misfortune to run out of petrol. Fuel was only allowed to be bought from this particular garage because, in those days, they gave out 'quadruple pink stamps' with every purchase and woe betide the assistant vet who didn't hand these over to the boss' wife who was an avid saver of them so that she could eventually cash them in for luxury items!

The practice area was probably about 35 miles in length and 25 miles in width and contained a number of 'branch' surgery premises in various towns therein. Animals, mainly dogs and cats, would be transported to the main surgery from the branch surgeries each morning in order to undergo various operations and were then returned that same evening to their owners at the premises from which they had been collected. Hence the reason for the cage in the car.

Cats weren't a huge problem to transport since they would be in wire cages. Most were pretty unhappy travelling in a vehicle, and they usually wailed and cried for the whole journey! Of course, they usually added a little bit of extra atmosphere to the cacophony in the car by urinating or defecating in their wire baskets! The majority of their cages had wire-mesh bases which inevitably meant that their excreted/evacuated bodily contents seeped through them and despite layers of newspapers on the car boot floor, they became dispersed and distributed throughout the area. Many of the patients were tomcats which were going to be neutered and one can only imagine the levels to which the powerful aroma within the car could reach!

Transporting dogs wasn't an awful lot less odorous, since few people took them a proper walk in the morning before presenting them for their operations. Bowels and bladders gave up the unequal struggle of a nighttime's containment and together with the morning distress whilst travelling, they too frequently released their copious contents!

The only way that one could keep some sort of peace between various dogs when they were in the cage was to tie them by their leads to the sides of the cage. This ensured that they didn't savage each other on the journey and probably more importantly it stopped them escaping when the rear cage doors were opened, and when each animal tried to make a swift exit in a vain attempt to gain its freedom!

The events of a really wet, November evening have become permanently etched in my mind. The rain was teeming down at the rate and force it often does in Scotland and the roads were flooded.

I had a house call to do on the way to my evening surgery after which I was hoping to re-unite five large dogs, of various breeds, with their owners. The house call was accomplished speedily and as I dashed back to the car, to my absolute horror, I noticed that the car had a flat tyre! Not just a soft semi-deflated tyre but a completely and utterly flat one! The car was un-driveable, and the only solution was to change the flat one for the spare tyre. Not exactly an exciting prospect having to do it in the cold, wet rain!

The first problem was locating the spare tyre, which had to be, of course, under the floor of the car boot; the boot with the cage on top of it!

There was no alternative but to try and remove the cage from the car. The cage contained the five large dogs and so it involved quite a logistical feat, namely getting the cage out of the car via the rear door and lowering it onto the ground, whilst still safely containing the dogs. The gallon tin of petrol had to be preserved at all costs too! Fortunately, the dogs were all secured to the inside of the cage or else they would have escaped because the cage had no floor.

During a bit of difficult manoeuvring to get the cage out, because it was not only a tight fit but also very heavy, and because of the non-existent floor, I struggled to stop the dogs from escaping from under the cage as I lowered it onto the ground!

With a sigh of relief, I returned to the task in hand and lifted up the floor of the boot in order to retrieve the car jack and remove the spare tyre. A rather pungent, noxious "aroma" wafted up from the well in which the tyre was contained which fairly took my breath away! In all the years that the car had been owned, there had never been an occasion to use the spare wheel and during that whole time the car had carried many dogs that had just happened to forget all the rules of their house training whilst they were travelling in the cage.

The 'aroma' was coming from a sea of old and stale urine, much of which had become concentrated by evaporation over time and had become a pretty disgusting urine soup in which the spare wheel and tyre were quietly marinading! Yuk!

There was no alternative for me but to unscrew the retaining bolt and delve into the soup to get the tyre out. That was bad enough but even worse was the effect of the 'marinade' on the rubber for the tyre surface had gone all soft and gooey! At least it was still fully inflated!

So, I jacked the car up, removed the flat tyre and got ready to put on the spare tyre. By this time, of course I was thoroughly soaked, my hands were sticky and smelly, and I was a little disgruntled, muttering about just how bad life could be at times. I was cold, wet, extremely odoriferous, and very late for my next appointments at the branch surgery. Could life get any worse than this I wondered?

Well, what a stupid thought that was! Just as I was struggling to remove the punctured tyre, and no sooner had it gone through my mind, than I heard a strange scraping sound. It was the sort of noise that makes the hairs on the back of one's neck stand-up such as when one hears the scraping of fingernails across a blackboard! I turned round to see where it was coming from and, peering through the wetness on my spectacles, I could see the cage and its contents disappearing down the road!

Oh no! Life just had got worse, much worse! The five dogs obviously weren't too keen on the idea of being tied to the cage and having to stand by the side of the road in the pouring rain and so like a team of Siberian Huskies pulling a sledge they were marching, or should I say running, down the road. The cage of course had no bottom to it and so they were able to head for home, wherever that happened to be!

There was no alternative but to run after them, get hold of the cage and pitting all my strength against their combined traction, drag the cage back to where the car was. Somehow, probably by a combination of determination and bad humour I got the tyre changed, whilst at the same time holding onto the cage to stop it being dragged down the road once more.

By now, I was extremely wet since even wearing waterproofs, as one couches down and bends forwards, the rain inevitable runs down the back of one's neck and drenches one's clothes, I flung the punctured tyre and wheel into the wheel bay for there was nowhere else to put it.

Now to get the cage back in and we'd soon be back on the road again. Well, that's what I thought until I was faced with the reality of having to lift a heavy steel cage back into the car. It had been custom-made by a blacksmith and it had been made to last and was very solid! Getting it out had been difficult enough but the reality was that it had been a relatively straightforward procedure compared to returning the cage to its previous position whilst still containing the dogs.

With grit and determination and a superhuman effort I managed to lift one end of the cage onto the boot floor of the car at which point the five dogs saw it as their chance to escape from under the sides of the cage which, of course had no floor! Fortunately, they all tried to escape in different directions and didn't manage to tow the cage away. Somehow or another I eventually managed to stop them and by a combination of verbal and physical encouragement they eventually did a synchronised jump, still within the cage, back into the car! Phew!

Fortunately, all the dogs were successfully re-united with their owners a short time later. I'm pretty sure that they must have wondered why their animals were so wet. Perhaps they thought that they had all been washed after their operations? I was just extremely relieved that I hadn't lost any or even all of them!

House Calls

Graduates nowadays rarely do house calls, partly because their surgeries are so well equipped with everything that may be needed to treat an animal and therefore it makes sense for owners to bring them in; partly, also, because more people have access to transport now, and home visits are both time consuming and relatively expensive. However, the younger vets do miss out on the experiences, frustrations, dangers and sometime even the fun of attending peoples' houses.

"This is Braeview police office. Is that the vet on call? We would like you to attend a house in Upper Brackenbridge to put a dog to sleep. It is fairly urgent. Could you attend shortly?"

"Exactly what is the reason for the urgent visit?" I asked.

"I will give you the address. It is 29 Top Street. A German Shepherd dog has just badly savaged a neighbour's child and our officers are away escorting the ambulance to the hospital. The owners are there though and they know you will be coming. The child has sustained some really severe and life-threatening injuries, sadly."

"OK, I will be there as soon as I can," I replied and set off at great speed towards Brackenbridge which was about twenty minutes away by car. I didn't need to check my equipment because I knew that I had enough euthanasia drugs with me but I did wonder as I sped along the road exactly what I was going to be faced with! Treating unruly dogs, untrained dogs and vicious dogs was part of everyday life and each held its own challenge, but this dog sounded as though it was in a league of its own! I had been stopped for speeding a number of times in the past and my excuses weren't always accepted by the police officers, but this time I was armed with an excuse (or so I thought!) because I was on urgent police business!

As I turned into the street, I could see little groups of women who were all huddled together, engaged in earnest conversation, and as many more women were leaning out of their upper windows watching what was happening. I suspect their dreary lives had never been so exciting! Police and ambulances and tragedy all on their doorstep! There were no children to be seen however since they had all been shut away inside. I was regarded with a mixture of curiosity and I suppose wonderment that here was someone who was going to have to tackle the canine culprit. I could see them imagining that maybe I would end up needing an ambulance too.

"Are you the vet?" shouted one woman from across the street. "Just watch yourself, son, for he's a huge, big, bad bugger. We are all terrified of him. We've all told her that it's a surprise he hasn't already killed somebody! He needs putting to sleep!"

Reassuring words, indeed and just what I needed to hear as I approached the front door, clutching my medical case in front of me. I rang the bell and a cacophony of hysterical barking and growling interspersed with human voices shouting and cursing erupted. Nobody answered the door, so

I rang the bell again and knocked loudly on the door. The noise inside continued and eventually the door opened a tiny bit, just enough for me to see part of a man's face but also to see the shape of a large, hairy, manic animal leaping up and down behind him!

"What do YOU want?" he growled at me through the crack in the door.

"I've been asked by the police to come and put your dog to sleep," I replied. "I'm the vet."

"Oh right, I see. Well, you cannae come in the noo 'cos he's that wound up he'll kill you!"

"Well, I need to come in!" I replied, "Can you not just shut him in a room somewhere until we decide what we are going to do? You **do** know why I have come don't you?"

"Aye, I do," he replied, "and I think it's for the best but the wife is having none of it and doesn't want it done!"

He shut the door and I could hear him trying to get the dog into the dining room where his wife was wailing and screaming! I heard a door shutting and then he reappeared at the front door.

"In ye come then. He's shut in the back room. I really don't know how you're going to deal with him. The wife won't let you take him away!"

As I entered the dark hallway I glanced back over my shoulder and saw the gaggle of women now, somewhat bravely, gathering on the road outside the door. They were obviously intent on not missing any of the drama!

"Dinnae fancy his job after what yon beast did to that poor wee lassie." were the reassuring words that I heard from the pavement as I closed the door behind me!

The house was dark inside and I had to ask for some lights to be put on as I discussed the situation with the dog's owner. I must admit that it was slightly difficult to concentrate through the constant noise of growling and barking as the canine fiend hurled itself at the living room door in an attempt to get at this stranger in his house! With the amount of frantic scratching at the door, it surely wouldn't be long until he came right through it!

"Well. What are you going to do?" The man asked me.

"If you are going to be sensible about it, you know that he needs put to sleep. The police can't make you do it without going to court but their advice, in view of what has happened, is absolutely correct. If you are in agreement, I will just put him to sleep here in the house?"

"I am definitely OK with that," he replied, "I knew he'd savage somebody one day. We should have done it before but my wife won't agree. He's her baby and she has him spoiled rotten. I really don't know how we are going to do this though."

"Have you got a choke chain or a choke lead for him?" I asked somewhat hopefully and having received an affirmative reply I asked him if he could go and put it on the dog.

He managed to get into the dining room without the dog escaping past him and eventually after a bit of a scuffle I heard him shouting to me. "Right, in you come. I've got him now but I don't know how long I can hold him, he's such a wound-up, big bad beast!"

I could barely make out what he was shouting over the noise of the dog and because of the wailing and hysterical screaming of his wife. I opened the dining room door rather gingerly and carefully, getting ready to retreat if he lost his grip on this crazy hound who was up on his back legs, screaming at me, mouth wide open, drooling saliva and showing off all of his magnificent dental equipment! The nearest thing to confronting a Grizzly Bear!

The dog was pretty fearsome looking but was only marginally more frightening than the woman! To say that she was of rather large proportions would be an understatement! She was enormous, red faced, angry and hysterical.

"You're not taking him away! I won't have it! He didn't mean to bite her. She came past the garden gate that's all. I'm not having my baby put to sleep." And with that she started sobbing and wailing. "You are just not doing it! I won't let you!"

Her sobbing and general hysteria was making the dog even worse and I could sense by her husband's face that he was nearing the end of his strength and ability to keep hold of the dog. I had to do something quickly.

"Look here," I said to her, "I have been sent by the police to do it and your husband has agreed that the dog is going to be put to sleep. It's obviously extremely dangerous and next time it might actually kill a child! What is his name anyway?"

"Rebel!" was her answer and with that she threw her arms around the dog's neck, overbalanced and ended up falling on top of the dog, wailing and sobbing all the while.

Fortunately for me, it was the best thing that she could have done because Rebel was now pinned to the floor under the loving embrace of a twenty-plus stone woman who couldn't get up unaided! As she heaved and sobbed and wailed and tried to protect her beloved Rebel from me, I seized my chance and managed to extract one front leg from under her heaving body. Rebel had no chance of moving, and indeed was quite likely to expire before I could carry out the 'deed'!

I looked to her husband for final approval then quickly clipped some fur off Rebel's leg, raised a vein and injected the euthanasia solution. Rebel slipped away peacefully and I couldn't have been more relieved!

As I left the house the congregation of women were still outside. "Did you not manage to do it then?" one of them asked. "Did he not savage you? Can't believe you're unscathed!"

I couldn't quite believe it either!

My next encounter with a German Shepherd was not so much on a house visit as on a visit to a partially renovated flat!

The foreman of a construction company telephoned the practice requesting that someone would visit their current renovation project, which was a block of flats, because there was a problem with their guard dog. He didn't specify exactly what the problem with the dog was but he requested a visit as soon as possible, because whatever the issue was, it had been going on for over two days.

I arrived at the block of flats which was surrounded by scaffolding and went to find the foreman.

"Are you the vet?" he enquired. "I'm so glad that you're here. We haven't been able to get any work done for almost three days now."

"Why is that then?" I asked him, being completely unable to see the connection between a dog and the inability to get any work done. Perhaps the dog was ill and they were such a lot of softhearted builders that they were unable to work because of worrying about it? Hardly likely I thought!

"Well, it's like this. Three days ago, a chap asked us if we'd like a dog for the site since he was going off to Australia the next day. It seemed like quite a nice friendly dog and it stayed with us for the rest of that day and so we decided to keep him. We fed him and then shut him in one of the flats that we were renovating so that he could guard it for the night. However, when we arrived the next morning, he was really aggressive and none of us could get into the flat! He was ferociously guarding it!

The first chap who entered the flat was attacked and bitten so badly that he had to go to hospital. The next person who tried to get in ended up with a broken wrist and the boss has decided that enough is enough and he wants you to remove him. We are only able to open the door a tiny bit and he attacks us if we try and do anything. He has even snapped a brush handle that we were using for defence!"

This certainly sounded like a bit of a challenge. If it was as bad as described, then I would need to be careful and maybe it would be wise if I wore a bit of protection. "But what?" was the question! I donned my thigh boots, which I wore on farm calls, put on my heaviest jacket, picked up my medical case and a choker-lead rope then followed the foreman up a couple of flights of stairs.

"He's in there," I was informed as he pointed to a closed door, lying outside of which was an assortment of broken sticks and broom handles, most of which had deep teeth marks on them!

It was quite obvious that they had been used to either subdue the dog or as defensive weapons when they opened the door!

"I'll leave you to it then!" the foreman casually announced and then he rapidly disappeared!

So, it was just me and the mad German Shepherd. I opened the door a tiny fraction to be instantly greeted by a mouthful of teeth in the possession of an angry dog! What is more, he was launching himself at the door at throat height! Oh dear!

I had to work out a plan of action so that I could safely enter the flat and catch the animal but without letting him escape at the same time!

Taking a deep breath, and imitating an SAS soldier entering a terrorist's building, I kicked open the door and immediately entered the room. As expected, the dog immediately launched himself towards my throat area as I lifted up my leather case as a shield. His teeth sunk into the leather and then he fell back ready to launch his second attack! Without a moment's hesitation and with my most commanding voice I shouted at him and looked him straight in the eye. He hesitated for a slight moment and I moved forward towards him, maintaining eye contact with him!

"Sit down! You horrible dog! Don't think that you're going to subdue me!" I continued to advance towards him and a confused expression appeared on his face. He started to tremble a little and without losing my eye contact he reversed across the room, and I kept walking towards him. He retreated into a corner and started to shake really violently and then, unexpectedly, started to squirt urine. He was certainly a submissive dog now and without further ado I slipped a lead over his head and started stroking him and speaking in a kindly voice.

"Come on boy." He stood up and trotted out of the flat by my side like a well-trained dog.

The builders were totally in awe of my ability and skill at being a dog 'whisperer'!

"What are you going to do with him now? We certainly don't want him!"

"I will take him and re-home him. I know the ideal place for him."

I took him to a local man who ran a security firm and trained dogs for patrol work. Only a short while previously he had told me how he handled 'wild' Alsatians that had been tied up all their lives and were acting as very effective guard dogs. They hated everybody! His technique involved walking confidently up to them whist staring directly into their eyes and speaking to them in a calm but confident, reassuring voice and then slipping a lead over them. It never failed apparently!

Having heard his theory, I resolved to try it out if the opportunity ever arose. A short time after he had imparted his wisdom to me, I had a farm visit to do. I arrived at the farm and parked my car just out of the reach of a particularly nasty collie that was chained up outside. It was not much use as a working dog but was extremely effective as a guard dog. Its chain was just long enough so that the dog could reach the back door of the farmhouse. It was impossible to knock at the door without encountering the fangs of this creature.

There was no sign of anybody about the farm and I had a sudden thought that maybe I could put the dog-handling advice, that I had been given, into practice and see if it really worked!

I got out of my car and approached the collie which, by this time was standing on his back legs, teeth bared and snarling having reached the limits of his chain. As I walked towards him, I said, "Right you horrible dog, just stop this nonsense and calm down." At the same time, I stared intensely at him and confidently walked towards him as I continued talking to him in my most dominant voice.

To my great surprise, he stopped growling, got onto all four legs and as I approached him, he started reversing away from me and becoming quiet! This was wonderful I thought. The technique really works! He duly retreated the full length of his chain and as he reversed, I advanced towards him. Eventually he ended up in his kennel, started trembling and then began to pee himself. Totally subdued and submissive!

Wow! Was I not impressed with myself! I stood looking at him for a few moments and he continued to shake and be submissive. I turned around and headed back towards my car, feeling as pleased as punch with my new found skills! I hadn't taken more than three steps before this black and white dog exited his kennel with the speed of an Exocet missile and sunk his bared fangs into my rear end!

Ouch! The one piece of advice that I had not been given was 'never lose eye contact with the dog'!

Lesson learned!

On occasion, the humans in some houses were often scarier and crazier than the pets.

I was sent on a house call to see a cat that wasn't well. There was no indication of what the problem was, just that the cat wasn't well. I duly arrived at the address which was an upper flat in a two up/two down block of houses which had an external door and then a steep staircase leading up to the flat itself. I rang the bell, the response to which was a window being opened and a woman's head appearing through it.

"What do YOU want?" she asked in a fairly aggressive manner.

"I am the vet that you telephoned about your cat," I answered, holding my stethoscope and medical case in my hands.

"No, you are not!" was the answer.

"Yes, I most certainly am!" I replied and held up my case and stethoscope to confirm my credentials and added, "Don't you have a cat that is ill?"

She sorted of grunted and closed the window and a short while later she appeared at the front door. She only partially opened it, which was not unusual, since I imagined that she didn't want her cat to escape.

"Are you sure you are a vet?" She asked again. And after further reassurance she indicated to me to enter the stairway.

I expected her to go up the stairs in front of me but instead she let me pass by her and proceeded to lock the outer door behind her. I reached the door at the top of the stairs and turned around to ask her which way I was to go. She indicated that I was to turn right and then I was to head into the living room. As I entered the living room, I was aware of the lady locking the door at the stair head, not only with a key but with a hasp and padlock too!

I assumed that she lived alone and was quite security conscious, but this was a little bit weird to say the least. She must have some troublesome neighbours. I was standing in her living room, looking around to see if I could see her cat, when she entered and promptly locked and bolted the living room door. This certainly wasn't normal behaviour!

"Right, you're not taking me away again!" she suddenly shouted to me. "I know full well who you are and I'm not coming! I'm definitely not going back there!" By now she was screaming!

This was getting a bit concerning now because she had a mad, agitated look in her eyes and I fully expected her to produce a kitchen knife or similar!

"Go back where?" I hesitantly asked.

"You know! Don't humour me! I know where you're from! The hospital, of course! You're one of the doctors, aren't you? Come on, admit it!"

"Of course, I'm not one of the doctors! I'm the vet that you phoned up about your cat. See, I have my stethoscope and medical stuff to treat your cat. You do have a cat? Don't you?" I silently hoped that she definitely did have one! I was obviously now locked in with an ex-psychiatric patient!

It was in the days before we had mobile phones and I was now stuck in this flat with a deranged woman and with no means of contacting the outside world.

"Well, I'm just not coming with you. You're not taking me away again. There's no way that I'm leaving here," she repeated and then added, "Anyway, the doors are all locked and bolted and you can't get out!"

Showing her my animal drugs, my visiting cards, and anything else that I could think of that would confirm that I was a vet still didn't convince her. In retrospect possibly showing her my syringes wasn't my best move since that induced another paroxysm of screaming at me, "You're not injecting me with that stuff again! I'm not letting you! There's no way that you're getting me out of here! I just won't go."

Eventually I managed to get her to calm down and eventually, after about an hour, I managed to examine her cat, by which time she had forgotten why she had asked for a house visit! In fact, she insisted that she had never even phoned for a vet! There didn't seem to be too much amiss with the cat and I now needed to plan my exit without any mishaps!

Being locked in alone with a mad woman isn't exactly a fun way to spend your time! At one point, I thought she was going to threaten me with a knife but miraculously I managed to eventually talk her down to some sort of rationality! Persuading her to unlock all the various doors took a lot time and cajoling, Eventually, I was only allowed to leave because I suggested that I would see myself out, unlock the lower outside door and then once outside I would lock it and put the keys through the letterbox! In that way, she wouldn't need to come downstairs and then there was no chance of me taking her with me! Fresh air never smelt so good!

Well, life is what it is!

The tale didn't completely end there though because she kept turning up at my surgery with presents for me! I've no idea what her intentions were but that thought was even more disconcerting than being locked in a flat with her!

Humans were definitely more of a challenge than animals!

Drowning the Pine Snake!

One of the most exciting things about being a vet is that one never knows what is going to happen next when one is on call, nor what sort of patient one may be called to see. Clients phone up with perceived emergencies and most often, one has to drop whatever it is one is doing and attend to them which usually means that on a busy night on call, mealtimes, as others know them, doesn't exist.

This is particularly true if the practice covers a large geographical area, since the time travelling to and from calls can occupy a large portion of one's shift.

Late one evening as I was heading home, tired and hungry and looking forward to my dinner, my mobile phone rang. I stopped the car and I sighed as I answered it because it probably heralded yet another call-out.

An extremely agitated voice came over the airwaves, "Quick, quick you've got to come immediately, one of my snakes is trying to eat the other one and we can't get them apart. Help! Please! Please come quickly! It's really serious!"

I didn't recognise the caller's voice but I could sense that he was in a real panic. I tried to calm him down and attempted to get some more information from him about what was happening.

"Our two Pine Snakes were busy in the middle of mating and we thought that was ok but then the male one has started to eat the female one and now he is trying to swallow her! My wife tried to put a pillowcase between them but he started to swallow that too! Quick, quick you need to come quickly, my wife is in the bath at this very minute trying to drown them to get them apart!"

"Who is calling and what is your address?" I asked.

"It's Mr Harris," was the reply, "You know my wife, Mrs Harris, from seeing our python 'Tiny'."

Oh, wow! I thought to myself, the exotic Mrs Harris in the bath with snakes. *This I have to see!*

I had previously encountered Mrs Harris at our surgery premises when she brought in her python that wasn't eating and immediately remembered who it was and how little in the way of clothing she had worn. Now getting to see her in the bath, I reckoned, was definitely an experience worth missing my dinner for!

There was quite obviously a lot of panic going on in their household and so I turned my car round and headed, at top speed, to the address which was about 12 miles away. Never had that distance been covered in such a short space of time and I arrived at the Harris's home, hoping that Mrs H was still in the bath!

"Quick, quick, come quickly," her husband said as he ushered me up the stairs, "my wife is still in the bath and she can't get them apart!" I bounded up the stairs after him whilst inwardly wondering whether my breathlessness was due to my degree of unfitness or whether it was due to anticipation or perhaps just a mixture of both!

As we both burst into the bathroom, I immediately noticed Mrs Harris, who was sitting in a bath that was half filled with water, clutching two, rather intimately connected, mating snakes! One of them, the male one, had latched onto the other one's throat in some sort of serpentine 'love bite' which also involved a partly ingested pillowcase while still continuing the breeding act at the other end. Locked in a loving embrace hardly described the situation!

This, of course, was all taking place whilst they were partly submerged in a bath of water and while being valiantly restrained by Mrs Harris who was lying in the water with them and who was desperately trying to stop the male swallowing the female one! Through the mass of writhing 12-foot-long snakes I just happened to notice, in passing of course, that Mrs Harris was completely wet through…but was fully clothed! I could now give the snakes my full attention!

I took hold of the male snake by his upper neck and saw that he was, indeed, intent on eating the female one since his impressive array of teeth were latched onto the female's head through part of a pillowcase.

"Oh dear! I really think he's going to kill her," said Mrs Harris in a shaky voice, "I just can't get them apart."

"Let me see what's happening," was my reply as I tried to check how attached they really were. I gently tugged on the pillowcase which was lodged between them and then tried to detach one snake from the other. As I did so, the male suddenly let go of the female's neck and simultaneously detached himself from her lower region too!

"How in all the world did you do that? I have been trying to get them apart for ages!" was Mrs Harris's astonished question.

Two rather large snakes were now writhing freely in the bathwater, well almost freely for I made sure that I retained a hold on the male's neck.

We returned the culprits to separate vivaria and set about getting dried!

"I really can't believe how easily you did that! I had been trying for ages and yet, for you, they just jumped apart!" exclaimed Mrs Harris, "What exactly was your trick?"

I tried to suggest to her that if she had been involved in the same sort of activity as the snakes had been, then she, too, might have forgotten what she was doing if her dentist tried to examine her mouth!

"What did happen then?" I asked them.

It turned out that Mr and Mrs Harris had been watching the television when they heard a commotion behind them in one of their numerous vivaria. They thought that the two occupants were fighting and were quite concerned until they realised, by their activities, that the two snakes were writhing about and trying to copulate! Their concern changed to admiration and then apparently to envy, at least on the part of Mrs Harris, when they learnt that courtship and copulation itself could last from between two and twenty-four hours, according to their Pine snake manual! Obviously, it was way beyond the realms of her personal experience!

They settled down to watch the performance of the amorous duo since it was much more interesting and exciting than any of that evening's programmes on the tele! Their excitement rapidly changed to concern when they realised that not only were the snakes now successfully joined together but that the male had then begun to 'swallow' his partner! The 'book' hadn't said anything about that activity and that's when they decided that their beloved Pine snake was not only a talented lover but also had a cannibalistic fetish too! Panic had set in. They were unable to part them despite their best efforts, and they had tried to stuff a pillowcase between the snakes in an attempt to stop the female being eaten!

In an amazing flash of inspiration, they jointly decided that the only thing that might interrupt and stop this cannibalistic loving was to quickly fill the bath with water and to submerge the amorous, wriggling pair in the water. As they thrashed about, Mrs Harris could only restrain them by jumping into the bath with them whilst still trying to hang onto them and stopping further injury. Unfortunately, she didn't have time to take her clothes off first!

Whether Mrs Harris's preferred diagnosis of cannibalism was correct or just over enthusiastic love-biting going on, was open to debate but it provided a little bit of entertainment and yet again I had a late dinner! The journey home, however, was somewhat slower and at a more sedate pace than the one to the call out!

New Beginnings

Starting out on one's career can be both stressful and nerve wracking. I'm pretty certain that every new graduate has started their first job with a huge amount of trepidation! The capacity for self-doubt is enormous! If an animal comes in, will I know what it is? If I know what it is, will I know what is wrong with it? If I know what's wrong with it, will I know now to treat it? If I know the treatment, will I remember the dosage of the drugs? If I remember the drug, will I remember the side effects or contraindications of the drugs? Will I know how to feed it or look after it? Will I know its reproductive cycle or how to handle it safely? So many questions and doubts, not even mentioning in the pre-computer days having to remember the costs of the hundreds of drugs!

Then without realising it, a little bit of experience and confidence has been gained and one can look forward to the next patient with anticipation and even excitement. The new graduate is pretty obvious to most clients and although most are very pleasant, there are always some who never miss a chance to belittle the new vet! I can remember even being asked if I wanted to be a vet when I left school! That's about as sarcastic as one can be!

Changing practice has its own stress too with the necessity of finding one's way around an unfamiliar area, being accepted by new clients and, not least, getting along with the rest of the vets and nurses and fitting in with their working methods.

When I started in practice, it was the norm to be provided with a car and accommodation. On one occasion, when I moved to another area, a practice car wasn't immediately available and I was asked if I didn't mind using my own car for a week or so. That wasn't a problem since I had been used to using it in my previous job and I quite liked it anyway because it was very fast! So, I set off, finding my way about and having to prove myself to a new set of farm clients. My very first call was to an ewe that was having difficulty lambing and from which I successfully delivered two live lambs.

I didn't realise that it was a kind of test because the farmer was a cousin of the practice secretary and by the time that I had returned to the practice he had phoned her with his opinion on my abilities! The farmers' jungle hot line then swung into operation and it seemed that by the end of that day the whole community knew about the new vet in town! In that expressive way of the Highlanders, I became known as the vet with the yellow 'labor a dor' (not Labrador!) since I always took my dog with me in the car.

I just loved the area, the people and the work which usually entailed a succession of small visits to farmers and crofters seeing sick animals, castrating, dehorning and attending to cows having difficulties calving etc. On my very first morning, my boss asked me what I had on my wrist! I replied that it was my watch whilst thinking it was a really odd question!

"Well, you won't need that up here!" was his answer, "You will go out on your rounds in the morning and you'll come back when you've finished them and you won't worry about the time! No one does up here! These folks are the salt of the earth and you must never refuse their hospitality because you will cause offence. You can always make time for a cup of tea and besides they love to get your news.

If you are genuinely pushed for time or need to attend an emergency, then just tell them that you need to speed off but ask them to keep the tea in the pot for you and you will get it next time you are passing! That way, if you have time on your hands in the future or even if you're just in need of a cup of tea, then call in and ask them if they still have your cup of tea in the pot! They will be delighted and honoured that you called in to see them!"

Of course, I had to take his advice and, on a surfeit of hospitality, within a few weeks my weight had increased from that of a twelve and a half stone weakling to that of a fourteen and a half stone weakling! Unfortunately, it wasn't all an increase in muscle bulk either, although sawing through the granite-like horns of numerous Highland cows must have contributed something! In the Highlands and especially on the West Coast, the pace of life was slow and even the Spanish expression, 'Manana', meaning tomorrow will do, on the West Coast smacked of really indecent haste!

"There are some calves to disbud at Frasers Glenbrae. Could you go and do them this afternoon? They're nice people but they don't have much help. Mr Fraser, who you will like, is becoming quite infirm but you'll manage okay if you just take your time. Take the electric dehorning iron because John is using the gas one," were the senior partner's instructions.

I arrived at the croft and introduced myself and we started getting the calves ready for disbudding. I had usually been used to a gas iron or disbudding irons that were heated in braziers and which were very efficient, but this electric iron wasn't something that I was familiar with. It had short cables which were attached to the battery of one's car and this meant that the car needed to be parked, with its bonnet up, right next to the calf pen and each calf had to be manhandled out and dragged up to the car. I was slightly concerned that my car would get bashed during the struggles with the calves but, as it turned out, this was the least of my worries!

The dehorning iron was attached to the battery and the disbudding procedures begun, after the calves' horn buds were anaesthetised with local anaesthetic. The amount of heat that was generated in the iron was not very impressive and it struggled to get hot enough to perform a quick job. We were on our third calf when I turned round to see smoke emanating from the inside of my car!

Horrified I quickly opened the driver's door to get my dog out, who by this time was cowering on the back window ledge in an effort to get away from the smoke! Realising that there was some electrical problem I quickly detached the pretty useless disbudding iron and, fortunately, avoided the whole car going up in flames! My lovely car was now totally incapacitated since the whole wiring loom had burnt out! What a great start to a new job and using my own car into the bargain!

Apparently, this problem had never been known to have happened before, but the partners did admit that it was a pretty useless disbudding iron! They blamed the mishap on the funny electrical system of my foreign car! However, they managed to find me another old car to use for the rest of the week and I vowed never to use that disbudding iron ever again.

The next day I set off for a few visits to do some work in a variety of small crofts that were situated along an escarpment which was high above the local town. This geographical situation meant that it was colloquially known as 'The Heights'. The work was enjoyable, the people were nice and everything went according to plan and so I was really feeling quite pleased with myself after the traumas of the day before! No mishaps this afternoon!

I headed back to the surgery, enjoying the view and the scenery from this high vantage point and negotiated the narrow single-track road that linked the 'Heights' to the town below. However, before one could reach the town one had to descend down a very narrow road which had, arguably, the steepest gradient in the country!

It was absolutely essential that passing places, which were relatively infrequent, were used to allow cars to pass each other. The normal protocol was for the car which was nearest a passing place to pull over into it and thus allow the vehicle coming in the opposite direction to get past.

Selecting a low gear, I cautiously began my descent from the 'Heights'. I hadn't travelled more than a couple of hundred yards down the hill when I saw an old, somewhat battered looking car travelling up the hill. Instead of driving into the nearest passing place the driver kept coming on up the hill and just as I realised that the car wasn't going to get past me, the driver who was staring straight ahead, attempted to drive past my car, which, by this time I had driven as far into my side of the road as I possibly could. Unfortunately, it wasn't far enough! My lateral travel was impeded by a sturdy stone wall or dyke!

A horrible crunching sound of metal upon metal was the next thing that I was aware of as the old woman driver in the opposite car kept on driving up the hill and at the same time removing most of my offside doors and wings! She wasn't driving very fast and she never even slowed down nor stopped. She just continued up the hill with a fixed, glazed expression on her face!

I jumped out my car and shouted at her, which was a total waste of time because she continued her slow journey up the hill! I ran up the hill after her and shouted through her window to be rewarded with no response! As I then hammered on her window it dawned on me that the only way that I could stop her was to open her car door, switch off her ignition and try and get her to halt! This I duly did and then, finally I got a response!

"H-hey! Chuusst w-wh-hat are y-yoush d-doing?" she asked in an extremely slurred voice! She was as drunk as a skunk and could hardly talk, far less drive!

"What do you think YOU are doing," was my angry response. "You have just taken off the side of my car! You should have pulled into the passing place down the hill or at the very least stopped driving after you hit me! Right, I need all your details. You've ruined my car."

"I n-never even s-s-shaw you," was the reply. "You're not g-g-going to report me to the p-poliche are you?"

"Of course, I am!" I said. "You shouldn't even be driving. You are quite obviously extremely drunk!"

"Oh! P-pleashe don't do that!" she pleaded in her slurred voice then quickly added, "C-can we chust not shettle it between ush if you go behind the dyke w-with me?"

Well, that was certainly an offer that I had never had before, but I kind of got the impression that it probably wasn't the first time that it had been offered by her! There are some offers, of course, that one can refuse!

Having obtained her details, with difficulty I may add, I continued my way back to the surgery, totally mortified that I had had a second 'car incident' within three days of starting a new job. Fortunately, the car was still driveable and I arrived at the surgery with a huge amount of trepidation!

I somewhat gingerly recounted what had happened to my car and was anticipating some sort of reprimand or criticism. To my great misfortune, all the other vets were back from their rounds and congregated in the office when I came in.

With great embarrassment, I recounted my tale of woe and ended up telling them about the offer to 'settle it over the dyke'!

To my great astonishment, one of the senior partners burst into fits of laughter at this point and then said, "Oh! That would be Irene, the milk woman then!"

She quite obviously had 'previous' for giving out this offer and was well known! Irene was indeed her name!

Fortunately, I am pleased to say, in all the years that I was there, I never had another mishap with a vehicle! I never had any better offers either while I was in that practice! The car was replaced with a new one and I was eternally grateful that I had happened to meet Irene in an old car!

About 10 or more years later, after I had left that practice and had moved out of the area, I met someone who had been born in that part of the Highlands and as I recounted my story and before I had finished, she too laughed and said, "Oh! That would be Irene, the milk woman!"

Reputations can go before you and can carry far it seems.

Many, many years later, in a different part of the country, I had an extremely good client who had a dairy herd. He was a very forward-thinking sort of farmer and he decided that he wanted all his cows to calve between 1st of January and the 12th of March, in order that none of them would be getting milked in their 'dry period' in the weeks before Christmas.

This was similar to what farmers did in New Zealand apparently. Although this seemed like a great idea at the time, the reality was that nearly 300 cows calving in that short space of time meant that there were 300 calves to find accommodation for too!

The end result of being overwhelmed with calves was that every neighbouring farm that had spare buildings or barns, was coerced, by way of significant financial inducements, into taking some of these calves and looking after them. So far, so good for it seemed to be a reasonable solution to the calf-housing problem.

Unfortunately, many of the calves developed profuse diarrhoea and I made daily visits to the various farms to treat them. One of the venues wasn't so much a farm as a small holding with a large barn where the calves were housed in pens constructed from straw bales and looked after by the youngish wife of the owner, who worked elsewhere.

The daily visits involved driving to a small village and then turning into the farm lane in the middle of that village which then led to the small holding. The farm manager was usually there because he had to visit the calves daily too.

However, our visits didn't always coincide. The usual routine was to knock on the farmhouse door and the farmer's wife would then appear and give us a hand to hold the calves and to tell us which ones had been ill. I was aware that there was quite a lot of banter and innuendo between her and the farm manager, but ribald comments and behaviour were not an uncommon occurrence on some farms. I did suspect that he was a randy old goat though!

Our visits became less and less coordinated and one particular morning, when I arrived to see the calves, the manager wasn't there. I therefore had to go and knock on the farmhouse door.

"I'll be with you in a minute." I heard the voice coming from behind the farmhouse door, followed by, "I'm just out of the shower!" No sooner had she said that than the door swung open to reveal the farmer's wife standing in her bare feet and wearing a housecoat. Without further ado she opened the housecoat completely and asked me, "How about it then?" as she stood naked in the doorway, flashing her not inconsiderable assets!

Of course, I didn't stare for too long, but I do seem to remember quickly taking in the whole scene, being the observant person that I am! It was another offer that had to be refused, although it was almost certainly a better offer than the old milk woman's! I went out to the calf shed and awaited the arrival of the farmer's wife and we attended to the calves as if nothing unusual had taken place!

However, as I drove away that morning it dawned on me that the manager, who I often used to meet at the farm, had most likely taken to visiting when I wasn't going to be there. In fact, Gill, the farmer's wife, had almost intimated the reason, for he apparently found it really extremely rude to refuse offers like the one that I had just been given! An old Billy Goat indeed! Hmm!

I continued my daily visits over the next few weeks, and I never bumped into the farm manager on any of them. I never got any more offers and I didn't manage to 'unsee' what I had previously seen at the farmhouse door either!

Approximately two years later a client who bred dogs arrived for a consultation.

"Well, I haven't seen you for a long time," I said. "How are things with you?"

"Oh! But we have seen you!" was the reply. "We used to watch you going up and down the lane every morning, past our house, to visit Gill Barrowman."

"Ah! So that is where you live?" I responded. "Yes, I went up and down that lane almost every morning for about ten weeks to see sick calves."

"Sick calves?" she asked with a surprised look on her face. "Oh dear! There was us thinking that you were just another of Gill's male visitors. Do you know that there were men up and down that road all day long when her husband was at work, including the local doctor! We really thought you were 'getting entertained' up there too!"

I hastened to assure her that I wasn't visiting for any other reason than to treat sick calves, but was absolutely horrified to think that such an innocent situation could have been so badly misconstrued.

"I must admit, we were a bit surprised. We didn't really think that you were that sort of person!"

Unfortunately, for two years they had thought exactly that!

People Skills

Everyone in this world has different talents and personality attributes and there are some people, who totally lack 'people skills'. They maybe abrasive, downright rude, shy, or just taciturn and uncommunicative. I suppose it's a mixture of being a result of one's innate personality and one's social upbringing. There are some individuals, however, that seem to be able to get along with anybody and who have witty, outgoing personalities. One of my bosses certainly fell into the latter category and I learned a lot from observing his mannerisms. I came to the conclusion that he could 'get away' with saying just about anything to anybody, even though he was being critical of them as he spoke to them. The reason seemed to be because he laughed and made what was a serious comment to appear as though he didn't actually mean it! However, he always got his point across without causing offence! I suppose that he was one of the 'old school' veterinary surgeons whose attributes and character have mostly now been subsumed by society's fixation with political correctness! He was loved and greatly respected by the whole community.

One lovely, warm summer's evening in early August, I was 'on call', doing a bit of gardening and hoping for a quiet night.

I heard the phone ringing and went inside to answer it whilst wondering what the call was going to be about.

"You are first on call tonight, aren't you?" it was my boss with his usual cheery manner.

"Yes," I answered. "What is the call?"

"Well, you know those travelling people at Duffus Park? They are just off the phone and apparently, they have a horse that has just gone through a barbed wire fence, and it needs some suturing for extensive wounds that it has sustained. It must be pretty bad because, as you know, they treat most things themselves and rarely call us out. I'll come with you. It's a lovely night for working outside and anyway the craic should be good! I quite fancy a bit of entertainment!"

There were three, well known, families of Travelling Folks in our area and in those days, they were often referred to as the 'Tinks'. This was not, in anyway, a derogatory term but was more a term of respect or affection for these people who had descended from the respected Highland Tinkers. Tinkers were extremely skilled at making and repairing all things domestic and agricultural, and in addition were also useful for doing seasonal farm work.

Their way of life was somewhat different from that of the 'settled' people but in true Highland fashion they were left alone to get on with their lives. Live and let live, be kind and hospitable, treat everyone with respect and don't interfere seemed to be the ethos.

I set off in my car and picked Bill up at his home. "Got all your stuff?" he asked as he got in the car. "The wounds sound really quite extensive. However, with two of us, I'm sure that we'll soon be done!"

We soon arrived at the encampment where there were various caravans, bits of old metalwork, junk and broken-down vehicles lying about. In the far corner, surrounding a horse, stood an assortment of rather dishevelled males who turned around to look at us as we appeared.

"Evening gents!" Bill called out cheerfully and brightly. "Well, what entertainment have you got for us this lovely evening?" as he beamed at the rather glum faces on the group of men.

"It's our 'hoss' here," volunteered the most senior looking one. "She needs a wee bit of stitching."

"Let's have a look then," said Bill as we pushed our way through the throng.

"Oh! My goodness," he exclaimed. "A wee bit of stitching, eh?" as we both looked in awe at the yearling, Highland filly in front of us. She looked more like an anatomical specimen that had been dissected than a horse! Her neck was totally devoid of skin, her muscles were exposed, and she stood there quietly trembling.

Quite an awesome sight! There was relatively little bleeding and on further examination it became apparent that the skin from the neck area wasn't exactly missing but was lying in folds, like a discarded pair of pyjamas, around her knees.

"What in all the world happened to her?" Bill asked.

"Well, you ken, we wis breaking her so that we could sell her at the wool fair tomorrer and she jist took off and went right through yon wire fence. A wee bit spirit in her, ye ken. Well, the laddies here couldnae stop her and she's torn her skin. Can you fix her so that we can sell her?" the spokesman enquired and somewhat optimistically, I thought!

"You won't be selling her tomorrow!" my boss replied. "This will take some time to heal. Anyway, we'd better get on."

Turning to me he said, "Right, you can do the suturing and I will look after that anaesthesia," and then addressing the head Tink, "He's a better and quicker surgeon than me. I'll keep her asleep while we watch him suture her up. Can you get us loads of warm, clean water please because we will need to clean the wounds a bit? Make sure it's in a clean basin too!"

As one of the throng scuttled away to procure some water, we proceeded to anaesthetise the filly and got our surgical equipment ready.

The wound was absolutely enormous but, most fortunately, it was possible to stretch the folds of skin from around her knees and to appose them to the skin under her chin. Fortuitously, there was no skin missing and therefore there was a good chance of repairing the defect so long as there was sufficient blood supply left for healing, all should be well. Very fortunately, also was the fact that there was a very slight warm breeze which was just enough to keep the area's fearsome midges and flies away!

I started to suture the wound realising that it was going to take some time and involved a lot of suturing.

"Is this going to be expensive Mister?" asked one of the men.

"Why, yes indeed, I think it definitely will be," replied the boss in his usual jocular tone. "Two vets, an extensive wound, loads of suturing, lots of skill and all happening in an evening, out of normal hours too! Very expensive, indeed, I would think! And a valuable young horse too."

I knew by his tone that it was all just banter because I knew that he always treated people fairly and would do his best to keep costs to a minimum.

"Exactly how do you charge Mister? Is it by the number of stitches?"

"It depends," was the reply. "This is a big wound tonight and so I think we will definitely be charging by the number of sutures!" then turning to me, Bill said, "Can you not put them in a bit closer together? I am sure that you could fit a few more sutures in there!" All the while, knowing that I was spacing them all correctly!

A gruff voice came from over my shoulder, from one member of the entranced audience, "One at the top, one at the bottom and one in the middle. That'll do us nicely if you're charging by the number of stitches!"

The banter continued in quite a good-natured fashion and after about an hour, with an extremely stiff, sore back I eventually stood up to admire my handiwork, relieved that the skin was looking almost like normal now.

All that remained was to allow the horse to recover from the anaesthetic and to get her back onto her feet again. We administered some antibiotics and painkillers and then she stood up fairly quickly, albeit slightly unsteadily.

"There now! Good job done! She looks as good as new! All we need to do now is to get settled up and we'll be out of your way."

"You mean that you actually want paid tonight?" said the head Traveller. "Well, you see we wis going to sell her tomorrow at the fair and now we can't, so we don't have nae money. We're totally flat-stone broke."

I was wondering how the boss was going to handle this situation because if one didn't get paid at the time then one never got paid! Travellers didn't deal in accounts! Their whole life revolved around wheeler dealing and striking bargains. Cash was king in their world.

Bill never lost his cool because he knew that to argue or get angry meant not getting paid at all.

Just as this slight altercation took place and as the men were reiterating their lack of money, the caravan door opened and the 'lady' of the camp appeared. She was concerned about how her horse was and was wondering what we were discussing.

"I've just been telling the vet that we've no money, but he's expecting to get paid tonight!" volunteered the woman's husband.

"Aye, that's right!" she replied. "We have nane at all!"

I was wondering whether we had reached an impasse and was also wondering how Bill would resolve the situation.

"I've never met a woman yet who didn't have a purse!" said Bill as he addressed the woman.

"Och Aye, I've got a purse OK. But there's nothing in it!" was the rejoinder.

"Oh! Come on now, you must have something in it," Bill said in a quiet, pleasant, non-confrontational tone of voice.

"OK, but I've only got half a croon in it," said she, still using the term for 'old money'.

To my great astonishment I then heard Bill say, "Oh well if half a crown is all that you have got, then I suppose, in fairness, that's all that I can charge you."

The woman's weathered face was a picture as she broke into a toothless grin! Her grin wasn't as wide as those on the faces of her men though who were all beaming broadly! They'd got their horse fixed and it had cost them virtually nothing. Quite a satisfying result really!

However, with just the right amount of a pause, Bill then said, "OK, it's a deal then. Half a crown, if that's all you've got, but I will need to charge you the VAT though."

"That's OK mister we dinnae mind paying the VAT," laughed the senior Traveller as the rest of his gang smirked in a group behind him.

"Well, that's settled then," laughed Bill. I must admit that I thought that he had taken leave of his senses! Until he quickly added, "Half a crown plus a hundred-and twenty-pounds VAT!"

A momentary intake of breath from the assembled throng was followed by a smile. They knew they had been beaten at their own game. The oldest man went into his back pocket and produced the biggest roll of banknotes that I had ever seen and started to peel them off! "Have you got any change boss?" was his question as he handed over a couple of hundred-pound notes!

All in all, a satisfying and enjoyable night but most of all a great lesson in keeping your cool and humouring people, not being in any way condescending but also manipulating them without them realising it! I questioned, in my own mind, how many other people would have got paid at all in that situation or maybe only got paid after a nasty confrontation.

"Ah! Dr Robinson, do come in please." Bill smiled pleasantly as he ushered the ageing Psychiatrist, head of a local institution, into the consulting room. "And what seems to be the trouble today?" he asked. Dr Robinson was a very intense lady who kept a lot of cats in her home. She had the ability to know what her cats were thinking and could interpret their thoughts into human language.

Not only that, but she was able to commune with the spirits of her cats that had previously departed this earthly world and who would come back to visit her. Extremely pleasant, if not a bit wacky, but quite difficult to satisfy on the other hand unless she agreed with your diagnosis and assessment of a condition affecting her feline friends!

On visits to her home, she could make you feel quite inadequate and uncomfortable if you couldn't sense or see the ghosts of her deceased cats as they prowled around the living room, even jumping through open windows to get some ghoulish fresh air. One just had to 'go with the flow' and try and get on with whatever you were there for!

No matter how amazing your clinical skills might be, they counted for nothing in her mind, unless you were 'in tune' with the goings on in her feline-orientated life! What sort a vet were you if you weren't able to commune with her cats' spirits?

We often, perhaps somewhat unkindly, wondered how she got on with her human patients. Maybe they recognised a kindred spirit and thought she was one of them?

"Marmaduke has been telling me recently that he's having some oral discomfort," she announced, "and he asked me if I could bring him to see you. He says that he thinks that his tooth may have to be extracted. I do hope that you can help him?"

Marmaduke happened to be the top cat in her household and nobody, human or feline, messed with him! If they did so, it was at their own peril! So, it was with a sinking feeling and some trepidation that Bill approached the hissing object that Dr Robinson was cradling in her arms. It was well known within the Practice that she was good at communicating with her cats but was totally useless when it came to restraining them!

Even catching them to examine them was something of a feline rodeo if one did a home visit, often pursuing them over and under beds and wardrobes, because we vets didn't possess the necessary skills to communicate with them! The fact that she couldn't catch them either was immaterial!

During one of his hissing episodes, whilst still cradled in the good doctor's arms, Bill saw the cause of Marmaduke's problem. One of his upper molars was decayed and loose and would need to be extracted.

"Oh dear. Poor Marmaduke. He told me that he was having tooth problems. What will you need to do? Does he need an extraction? When can you do it?"

"Dr Robinson, we will do it right now for you, seeing as we have just finished our consults this afternoon. I'll ask James to help me. Has he eaten today?"

"No. Not today. He told me he wasn't really feeling like any breakfast today. That's not like him."

I was summoned to the consulting room where Bill was trying to extract an extremely reluctant Marmaduke from Dr Robinson's grasp as she clutched him to her not inconsiderable bosom!

"Give me a hand here would you please? Marmaduke needs a dental extraction and I told Dr Robinson that we would do it right now."

"I will just come with you," Dr Robinson announced, seeing as she liked to always oversee and direct proceedings, giving her advice and direction where none was needed!

As he wrestled Marmaduke from Dr R's grasp, he motioned to me that I should follow him through to the operating theatre. "Get rid of her," he hissed under his breath as she went to follow us through. Marmaduke was wriggling furiously in a determined effort to escape as we duly entered the ops room, with Dr Robinson still bringing up the rear. "What's she still doing here?" he growled at me.

Just then, as I entered the room with Dr R following, a little voice from behind me said, "Will I shut the door Mr Macdonald? Just in case Marmaduke escapes?"

"Oh! Dr Robinson!" was Bill's immediate, light-hearted reply. "What a really wonderful idea! Yes, you shut the door, with yourself on the **outside** and we'll all get along much better. Thank you!" and with that she left the room and closed the door. Bliss!

No offence was taken and our task was completed without mishap. Dr Robinson was soon delighted to be reunited with Marmaduke. "Oh Mr Macdonald. You are wonderful. Thank you!"

I was left with the same opinion. How did he always manage delicate situations without causing offence?

His talents didn't just extend to being diplomatic, but he was also quite capable of 'winding up' colleagues and students.

One of his partners, Campbell, who had been married for just a few years had a rather attractive wife who was known to be quite possessive of him and somewhat jealous of his interactions with other women.

After completing afternoon rounds, the person who was due to take the evening consulting hour usually managed to go home and get something to eat before it started. Tonight, it was Campbell's turn.

The telephone in the office rang and Bill answered it. "Well, hello, if it isn't the lovely Jane? What can I do for you tonight?" he asked.

"I was just wondering where Campbell was and whether he was coming home for his dinner before evening surgery?"

"Just a minute and I will check for you. Let me see now," he said as he perused the visits book. "He went away in the early afternoon to do a visit. I think it was to the farm owned by that lonely, attractive, young widow at the other end of the practice. No! I wouldn't expect him back anytime soon. In fact, he'll probably be away for hours yet!" And he chuckled as he said it knowing what effect it was having on Jane. He could almost hear the steam coming out of her ears as she slammed the phone down!

Campbell, who had been in another room, appeared in the office and announced that he was nipping home for his tea before evening surgery. "Oh. By the way, who was that on the phone just now?" he asked.

"It was just your wife, Jane. She wanted to see if you were going home for your tea. I think she's got something 'hot' for you when you get home!" he replied chuckling to himself. The reception that Campbell was going to receive when he arrived home to be confronted by his enraged wife could hardly be imagined, but it would certainly be hot! Poor Campbell!

Another thing that Bill was good at, apart from teasing people, was getting information out of people without them realising that he was looking for it, often to their great embarrassment!

At that time, the practice consisted of five male vets and one female vet and sometimes the conversations could be quite agricultural and laddish! A certain amount of banter was normal and made it a happy place to work in. During University holidays we usually had students doing their clinical, extramural studies with us. In those far off days, the majority were males but there was an increasing number of female students too.

Eight o'clock on a Monday morning and a female student arrived in the office to begin her two-week placement. Carol was welcomed in and introduced to the staff and after a few pleasantries, the partners began to work out the day's 'rounds' for each vet and to decide which round would be the most beneficial for the student to go on.

"Did I hear you sneeze there?" Bill asked Carol.

"No. I didn't sneeze," she replied.

"Oh. I thought maybe you had a cold coming on?" Bill queried.

"No! I don't have a cold," was the reply from a somewhat confused Carol.

"Well, I just wanted to say that if you did have a cold then don't take ampicillin for it, because it stops the 'pill' from working."

"But I'm not on the pill," Carol quickly replied with some indignation.

"Oh! That's fine then," Bill responded. "That's all we needed to know. We know where we are now! Can't let you go out with all these young virile vets then. You'd better just come with me!" and then chuckled away to himself. No need to ask a direct question to get an answer and never miss an opportunity to embarrass someone or to 'pull their leg'.

Every one of us was on the receiving end of his mischievous 'humour' at some point or another. I will never forget Bill answering the phone and when he realised it was my fiancé on the call. I was sitting next to him, not knowing who he was speaking to and only heard one side of his conversation.

"Who did you say you were? Margaret? I just don't know! I can't keep up with these young lads. Do you know there are young women phoning up here every other day looking for him? We've had Mary, Janice and Jennifer already this week looking for him. What did you say your name was? Oh. Margaret? Margaret, I see. You must be another new one. Never heard of you before!"

Then he handed me the telephone saying with a broad grin. "It's for you! I think Margaret wants to speak to you!" And didn't she just want to do that!

The Things People Say

We all occasionally make mistakes when we speak and I am certain that in many walks of life people will have amusing stories of incidents where words or phrases have tumbled out that have not always been what the speaker had intended to say. Sometimes, of course, it was exactly what they meant to say but they had picked the incorrect words or pronunciation. I hasten to add that clients were never laughed at or ridiculed, for, as I indicated, we all could be capable of malapropisms, but in retrospect, some of the conversations could be amusing. Some hilarity was certainly caused by the only veterinary patients that could speak; namely parrots. We all know that some birds are capable of speech but, as a vet, there is something quite disconcerting about a patient that suddenly talks to you. There must be many people who have regretted either teaching their birds inappropriate words or being a bit careless with their language in front of these renowned mimics, which are accent and word perfect every time!

It is often through either stress or embarrassment that incorrect words or expressions come tumbling out! These have varied from the young boy whose dogs had, what he described as, swollen 'tentacles' to the gentleman who had obviously referred to a dictionary so that he could use the correct anatomical description of his male dog's anatomy, the 'Penn is'. Inwardly, there was a strong inclination to ask "where's that then?" but that would have been both unthinking and cruel.

Describing parts of animals' anatomy with vernacular terms wasn't a problem to many though and on one occasion a girl apologising for not being able to describe her young dog's problem, said, "This is really embarrassing. I don't know what to say." When asked what the problem was, she, without even a trace of embarrassment, announced, "His baws havenae drapped!"

Reproductive equipment and its description have a dictionary all of their own. Euphemisms were many and varied. The crude vernacular ones that are in everyday use by some sections of the population I won't repeat. At least with those words you generally knew what people meant! Being told that there's something wrong with his "How's your father" or "He's needing his back teeth taken out" (castration or neutering!) could be open to any interpretation but dentistry certainly wasn't what was being requested! Only a shy bachelor could have described a female dog as having "something wrong with her, er, um her" with an embarrassed cough, "her Vageeena!"

Neutering animals is part and parcel of everyday life for the majority of veterinary surgeons and once again I have heard many terms for the various operations. "I want him neuted!" Or, "I want you to mute him," were not uncommon expressions. One lady who appeared with a mature Jack Russell I will never forget. She was definitely a woman on a mission and wasn't interested in a discussion about castrating her dog for she said emphatically, "I just want him fixed and

I want him fixed right. I am fed up of him marking his territory and always escaping on the 'randan'. He must have fathered half the dogs in the area!" Before adding, with further emphasis and vehemence, "Small dogs, small men, they're all the same. They are all over sexed!" Obviously, she had personal experience! I just hope the dog wasn't being sent for surgery because of some of the demands being made on the owner in a tense domestic setting!

Perhaps my favourite expression came from the lips of a shy, rather demure, unmarried old lady who enquired in a whisper, "Do you think that you could make my tom cat into a bachelor, please?"

That request certainly made me wonder what her take on single, unmarried male life was!

For some reason, it seemed to be much easier for ladies to discuss spaying or neutering of female animals, presumably because they were more familiar with gynaecological matters. Hysterectomy was a term that was not uncommonly used, as was "I want it all taken away" or her "lady bits attended to"!

Anatomical parts of the female animal had as many different terms used to pinpoint which bit of the body the owner was talking about. Having 'woman's trouble' or problems with 'her front passage' were easily interpreted as were 'her lady bits' or the cutest of all, "something wrong with her, er, er, er her wee…fluffy."

One client, who was quite a robust sort of character and had no problem swearing like the proverbial 'trooper' was incredibly shy when it came to expressing herself about body parts. I assume that she was much more at ease with agricultural or automotive machinery because she described her female dog as having a, "Discharge from her, er, er her

Volvo," and then added, "I think that she needs her gearbox taken out." That certainly was the first time that I had heard a hysterectomy called that!

Shyness about parts of anatomy and reproductive activities wasn't just restricted to pet owners. Many farmers are actually very shy about discussing these things even though they dealt with them every day. This was especially the case when they spoke to lady receptionists. One farmer was heard to phone up when his bull was having some sort of problem with his genitalia and when he was asked exactly what was wrong, his garbled response was, "He's, err, err, ahem, lame. Just send a man!"

Vets are governed by rules and regulations like the other medical professions, and it necessitates giving regular check-ups to animals that have chronic conditions and that are on regular medications. Medications can't be prescribed unless animals are examined and the fact that the pet may experience the same symptoms some months or years later does not mean that the owner can just get a repeat prescription without the animal being seen.

Mrs Smith was a pretty forceful character and never 'minced her words' but on the other hand was usually a quite respectful and grateful client. However, one day she asked for a repeat medication for her guard dog which had a mouth infection. She was none too pleased when she was informed that she would need to get the dog examined again because it was many months since it had last been seen.

"Absolutely…bleep bleep…ridiculous," was her parting comment as she put down the telephone. I don't know whether her problem was that she didn't want to have to spend money on a consultation or whether the prospect of loading a dirty, hairy, somewhat aggressive German Shepherd guard dog into her nice clean car was just too much to contemplate.

Her appointment duly happened and she entered the consulting room with her dog. Between us, we managed to get the dog onto the table and I proceeded to look at his mouth while he too expressed his displeasure at being in the surgery! Tyson had experienced mouth infections previously and once again he had exceptionally inflamed, infected and sore gums.

As I was examining him, his owner, Mrs Smith, kept up a running commentary about her disgruntlement regarding being forced to bring the dog in, her face becoming more and more red, in fact, almost scarlet!

"Just exactly why should I need to bring him in? All I need is some penicillin," she asked. "You have seen him before, he's difficult to handle in here and anyway I know exactly what is wrong with him!"

"So exactly what **do** you think is wrong with him then?" I asked as I looked up and noticed her increasing annoyance and agitation. Her head was not only red but it was bobbing up and down with anger!

She spat out her words in a way that even a spitting cobra might have been proud of!

"Just like before, his mouth is full of nasty little orgasms and all I need is to get some penicillin to cure them!"

It was difficult to keep a straight face, because Mrs Smith didn't realise what she had said but on the other hand my nurse did hear it very plainly and was virtually doubled up with silent laughter. All that I was aware of was her saying under her breath, "Oh! What a lucky dog! A mouth full of little orgasms! Mmm!"

I had a difficult job resisting the temptation to say, "There's the penicillin Mrs Smith, that should sort out your little orgasms!"

Phone Calls and Chinese Whispers

"I need to speak to the vet who deals with the erotic animals."

Phone calls were sometimes very interesting, entertaining and were not always as expected. Some had unexpected twists, starting out as an apparently serious enquiry and degenerating into an obvious case of the caller getting some sort of sexual gratification on the other end of the line!

One such call started off as an apparently serious enquiry as to how birds mated. With question after question, the caller's breathing became heavier and heavier on the other end of the telephone line and it became apparent that this female caller was becoming somewhat excited! I had been trying to answer all the many questions with seriousness and professionalism until the breathless, panting voice stuttered, "Do you think that they get any pleasure from it?"

It dawned on me then why she wanted to speak to the erotic vet! It was time to terminate the call without getting deeper into the love life of birds and without causing offence. "Pleasure? Oh, I didn't know that there was any pleasure in that activity. I thought it was just something that males had to do out of a sense of duty!" All I heard was the phone being slammed down!

"Can you tell me if my bitch has been mated?" asked the caller.

"What makes you ask that?" I replied. "It could be difficult to tell you that over the phone. Is she in season and has she been with a male dog?"

"Oh yes, she's been in season for about 10 days."

"Have you a male dog?"

"Oh yes! I left them when I went off to the shops and he was locked in his cage but when I got back, he was chasing her around the kitchen. I really need to know whether she has been mated because she's only eight months of age!"

I replied, "Well, in that case I'm pretty certain that she will have been mated."

"How can you possibly say that?" was the anguished response.

"Because she was at the height of her season and he didn't burst out of his cage for no reason!" I replied with certainty.

"Well! I don't know how you can possibly say that," was the response. "He is her brother and I'm sure he wouldn't have done that!"

"Male dogs don't worry about things like that!" I told her. "They will definitely have been mating."

"Anyway, I couldn't see any…evidence," was her reply.

I thought it was probably a little bit indelicate to enquire about exactly what evidence she was expecting to see! "I'm certain that they will have been mating, evidence or not."

"Well, I don't see how she could possibly have been mated," responded the caller, "because she still had her pants on."

"Still had her pants on?"

"Well, yes, she did have. I didn't have any doggy pants so I just put a pair of mine on her. They fitted her quite well. Oh dear! This sounds awful."

"Was she still wearing them when you came home?"

"Oh yes! She still had them on."

"Well, in that case, I'm pretty sure that she hasn't been mated then," I replied.

"What did you say? A minute ago, you were absolutely certain that she had been mated and now you're telling me that she hasn't been. How can you now be so certain of that?"

"The thing is that you never told me about her wearing the good fitting pants until later in the conversation and you confirmed that she was still wearing them when you came home."

"Well, I was a bit embarrassed about telling you that they were mine," she said. "I still can't understand how you can now be so definitely certain that she hasn't been mated!"

"It's just that if they had been mating when you were out, I can't really see her managing to get dressed again afterwards! Can you? Bring her down and I can check for you though if you are still worried."

She politely declined that offer and went off the phone. As I put the receiver down, I turned around to find that some of my nurses had been listening into my side of the conversation, to their considerable amusement!

"You asked the wrong question there," one of them volunteered. "You should have asked her if they were both sitting back having a fag when she came in from the shops! That would definitely have clinched it!"

Asked in the light of her own personal experience obviously!

Everyone has their own view on life and some people can see things in a completely strange, different and often unrealistic light to the rest of us. I would never doubt the sincerity and intensity of their compassion and views, but they can often be a little bit 'off the wall'!

"I need to speak to a vet urgently, preferably one that knows about tiny animals," said the caller. "I'm really quite upset and distressed."

"OK, hang on a minute and I will see if one of the 'exotic' vets is free," replied the receptionist.

She then informed me that she had a really distressed and upset woman on the phone and asked me if I could speak to her and she smirked as she put the caller through to my phone. Strange behaviour I thought and unlike that receptionist.

"What seems to be the problem?" I asked the caller who replied in an agitated voice. "I need some antidepressants!"

"Antidepressants? Well, we can't give those out to you. Anyway, what seems to be your worry?" I said as kindly as possible in case she was feeling suicidal or similar.

"They're not for me!" she replied with indignation. "I don't need any. There's nothing wrong with me! They are for my slug."

"Slug?" I stammered and then began to wonder what sort of slug she could own. Maybe it was some exotic, tropical, coloured slug. It certainly was a new species for me if that was the case!

"So, just how do you know that he's depressed?" I gently asked her, not knowing anything about the psychiatric problems of slugs myself, and maybe hoping to pick up some useful information!

"Well, it's really quite obvious," she retorted. Obviously wondering how an experienced vet couldn't possibly know the answer to that dumb question.

"He really needs those antidepressants soon for he's fading fast. He's hardly moving about any more and his feelers (antennae) are drooping down. I am so worried about him. His mate, Sally, died last week and since then he has stopped eating and is going downhill fast."

Maybe this lady was an expert breeder of an exotic variety of slug? I decided to tread carefully and not reveal my relative ignorance about slug breeding! I was beginning to be slightly impressed with her knowledge of slugs and her ability to sex them when they are generally all hermaphrodites anyway!

"So, what happened to his mate?" I asked her.

"I don't know," she wailed down the phone. "But they were really truly bonded and fond of each other. The poor wee soul. Simon needs help quickly before he dies too. He's so lifeless, lethargic and he's off his food. I'm sure if we can get him out of his depression then he will be OK."

I had never been confronted with this scenario before, and before I started to consider drugs and doses etc., for depressed slugs, I needed some more information. I was also ethically and legally obliged to examine the slug before prescribing any medication.

"Can you bring him in then so that I can examine him, please? We will need to try and find out what is wrong with him first."

"And just how am I supposed to bring Simon in? The travelling might kill him in his present state."

"Well, just bring him in within his living container. It can't be too big surely."

"Don't be stupid! How can I do that? He lives in the garden."

"The garden? He's a garden slug?" I asked, a little bit taken aback. All thoughts of exotic slugs dashed!

"Yes, Simon and Sally both lived in my garden and were the best of friends. I know the bereavement has got to him and he's depressed and grieving!"

Well, she never did bring the slug in and I never got to exercise my slug psychiatry!

Misunderstandings and mixed messages do happen from time to time.

I once got a call to go and see a goat that had been in a road traffic accident.

I made my way there with some degree of haste and screeched to a halt in the farmyard.

"My, you were quick! I didn't expect you to be here quite so soon," said the farmer.

"I came as quickly as I could," I replied. "Now where is this injured goat?"

"Injured goat?" he queried.

"Yes. The one that was hit by the car," I responded.

"Nay lad, no car accidents here. Perhaps you've got the wrong place?"

"No, this was the farm I was told to come to. Do you have a goat?" I asked him.

"Yes, we've got a nanny in the byre over there that's got mastitis. I just phoned your surgery a few minutes ago."

So, we went across the yard to the byre and there was a nanny goat with a couple of bleating, hungry kids.

I examined the goat, confirmed the presence of acute mastitis and duly treated her and gave him advice about feeding the kids until the mother was better. I still couldn't work out why I had got a message about a road accident though!

It all became clear later when I questioned the person who had received the call and then passed it onto to another staff member who had then telephoned my wife who had subsequently relayed the message to me.

'My goat has kidded and has got a sore udder' became a Chinese whisper of mishearing and misunderstanding! It was translated into 'my goat has skidded and hurt its udder', which on the next relay became, 'the goat has been hit by a car (presumably a skidding one!) and has hurt its udder'! Hence the road traffic accident description! However, no harm done and the goat recovered thanks to her extremely prompt treatment!

On a Sunday morning, on another occasion an old lady, who had once upon a time been an actress, phoned to ask for help with her cat that wasn't well. She had a rather strangulated, upper-class accent and one had to listen very carefully to deduce what she meant. In addition, her old phone crackled with a lot of background noise when she spoke which made hearing her even more difficult. In addition, she had an entourage of large, barking dogs in the house which contributed to the lack of clarity when she phoned.

"My cat isn't very well this morning and she can't stand. I need a visit to see her this morning as quickly as the vet can manage."

"Well, the vet is out on his calls at the moment so why don't you bring her into the surgery yourself? It would be the quickest way of getting her attended to."

"And just exactly how do you suppose that I'm supposed to do that?" she said with some indignation.

"Well just pop her in a basket and bring her over," was the bright reply.

"And just EXACTLY how am I going to get a COW into a basket?" was her exasperated answer! "I need a visit!"

Point taken!

Rapport with Clients!

To be a successful general practitioner, it is essential that one has the ability to be able to develop a relationship with both the client and their pet. Usually, it is based on the client having faith in the veterinary surgeon and his abilities to handle and relate to their pets and not infrequently, long-term clients become friends. Working days pass much more nicely if the clients are pleasant and that there is humour or maybe some gentle banter during consultations. If clients do not feel intimidated and can feel that they can talk freely to their vet, then they sometimes unburden themselves of problems in their personal lives and not infrequently ask questions about their own medical problems, about which they don't feel comfortable asking their own doctors!

These are not diagnostic questions but are often questions about medical results that they didn't quite understand or queries about cancer diagnoses which they were too shy or felt too intimidated to ask their doctors. I suppose we should be honoured that we are confided in so frequently and I suspect that it is mainly because of the more relaxed relationship in the vet's consulting room. A good sense of humour gets everyone through difficult times but there are some individuals in life that just don't have this attribute!

Mr Mackenzie brought his rather cantankerous fox terrier, Rascal, to enquire about his eye problem. Rascal wasn't a patient that I saw frequently because I suspect that his owner felt that it was always a bit of an ordeal bringing him since he, Rascal, had a dislike of vets; me in particular! Mr Mackenzie seemed to be a reasonably jocular sort of person who always made some sort of amusing or, more often, caustic, sarcastic quip!

I got used to his 'sense of humour' and I suspect that he thought that his comments were really witty and funny. They were usually delivered as he went out of the door as a kind of parting shot! I laughed politely on most occasions and then went back to counting my fingers to make sure that Rascal hadn't bitten one off, for I suspect that was his avowed intention!

Rascal had a sore eye for a number of days before he appeared at the surgery because not only did Mr Mackenzie find it difficult to control his dog, he was pretty averse to being parted from his money too! He had hoped, rather unsuccessfully, that the eye condition would get better by itself.

With a struggle and at the third attempt, Mr Mackenzie managed to finally get Rascal onto the examination table. The next thing that had to happen was for me to examine his right eye which was tightly closed. The eye was obviously very painful and not surprisingly Rascal didn't want me to look at it. However, with much struggling and growling from Rascal and a few 'choice' expletives from Mr Mackenzie, who had the unenviable job of trying to keep Rascal's mouth shut, I managed to instil some anaesthetic drops into the affected eye.

The drops normally take effect pretty quickly but I decided to let Rascal calm down a little and to allow Mr Mackenzie to get his breath back before round two commenced. This entailed examining his eye with an ophthalmoscope and then applying a staining compound to his cornea to check for any surface damage or ulceration.

As we waited for a couple of minutes and chatted, I couldn't help thinking that the old adage about people looking like their dogs was indeed true! Mr Mackenzie had one of the longest noses that I had ever seen, and he did actually look quite like his fox terrier pet! The only advantage of his dog having a long nose was that it gave Mr Mackenzie something to wrap his hand around when he was restraining Rascal for examination. I'm not certain if Mr Mackenzie's own proboscis had any advantages over a standard size nose though!

Corneal damage and ulcers often heal relatively slowly, and the nearer to the centre of the cornea, the slower the healing is. As I instilled the staining drops into Rascal's eye it immediately became obvious that he had a huge ulcer right in the very centre of his eye! I communicated this news to Rascal's owner and emphasised the seriousness of the condition and how painful it would have been for Rascal.

He was none too pleased to be told that if he had brought him in earlier, then the ulcer might not have been so extensive and Rascal wouldn't have endured so much discomfort. In addition, the news that he would have to come back regularly until the ulcer had healed added to his annoyance. In fairness to him, though, the prospect of putting drops into an intemperate and unpredictable dog's eye four times a day must have been a bit worrying.

I demonstrated how to instil the drops and then opened the door to let them both leave. Mr Mackenzie, being the 'witty' person that he was, always had to have the last word and he informed me that it was perfectly obvious that I wasn't a 'dog whisperer'!

What a cheek! I thought to myself as I had no doubt that Rascal couldn't be easily examined by even the best doggie behaviourist! However, we were to see him back in a few days and depending upon satisfactory progress in the healing of the cornea we would need to see him back at least once weekly for the next 3 to 4 weeks. If the cornea wasn't healing, then we might have to admit Rascal for other procedures under anaesthetic.

I knew that this news wouldn't be well received and I fully expected that this possibility might come to pass. However, I also knew that Mr Mackenzie was extremely attached to his money and that he would make a determined effort to get those drops into the dog's eye so that no extra expense was incurred!

All credit must be given to Mr Mackenzie because he faithfully treated the dog's eye and healing began to take place. As expected, the healing progressed steadily and slowly but at the same time Rascal became more aggressive and more difficult to handle! Mr Mackenzie never missed a chance to make a cutting remark about my abilities but I just let them wash over me.

On what turned out to be the final visit the nurse ushered Mr Mackenzie into the consulting room and he didn't look particularly happy. I couldn't help noticing that he had a black eye and a sticking plaster on the very end of his rather large nose. Apart from in cartoons, I have never seen an Elastoplast applied in that manner, for two pieces had been applied and they were in the shape of an X.

Rascal no longer had a painful eye and he was on top form, jumping about and growling and full of terrier attitude! I could tell that it was not going to be easy to examine his eye on this occasion since his behaviour had been getting worse and worse at every visit. Mr Mackenzie managed to pick up the wriggling, snarling bundle and put him on the table from which he immediately tried to jump down.

With the help of the nurse, reluctant Rascal was restrained and I bent forward to examine his eye. I needed to be really close to his eye and as I looked through the ophthalmoscope all I could see out the side of my eye was a snarling, curling muzzle and an array of white teeth that were flashing and gnashing as he tried to get his own back on his least favourite person! Mr Mackenzie was valiantly trying to keep Rascal's mouth closed with his hand around the muzzle. There was nothing unusual so far because Rascal was always a difficult patient but that night, apart from noticing and avoiding the gnashing teeth, I just couldn't help keeping looking at the X plaster on the end of Mr Mackenzie's nose!

With considerable relief, I announced that Rascal's eye had now healed and he didn't need to come back. As he was paying his bill and as I was waiting for his usual witticism, I couldn't help myself by satisfying my curiosity about the strange plaster on his nose.

"Well, what happened to your nose then?" I enquired.

Without a trace of a smile, he replied. "If you had been a better vet and if you had got Rascal's eye better more quickly then he wouldn't have got so fed up and bad tempered, with me putting drops in his eye, and he wouldn't have bitten me on my nose!"

That comment was no more than I would have expected from him and I did certainly feel slightly aggrieved by it since I knew that Rascal's eye had healed up exceptionally well and within the predicted time scale. I wasn't going to let Mr Mackenzie have the satisfaction of knowing that his comment was hurtful and so I kind of laughed and said, "Oh well, it could have been worse!"

"What do you mean it could have been worse?" he retorted, rather sharply.

I knew that he expected me to reply in the traditional manner by saying, "It could have been worse because it might have been me that he had bitten."

Perhaps, subconsciously, I had been waiting for a chance to get my own back after having suffered a few weeks of his verbal sarcasm, but for whatever reason the reply that tumbled out was, "Well it could have been much worse." Before pausing slightly and then continuing with, "He could have bitten somebody that was good looking!" Absolutely no offence was intended and I laughed as I said it so that he knew it was a jocular comment.

I really thought that he would have some witty or sarcastic reply as he usually liked to have the last word, perhaps calling me a cheeky swine or something similar. Not this time, however! With a withering glance at me he picked up Rascal and departed, never to be seen again! Hmmm, it just goes to show that some people can dish it out but they can't take it themselves!

I have come to realise that there are some things that you shouldn't tease people about or make jokes about in Scotland;

namely, politics, religion and especially football! The tribal and sectarian allegiances are both deep and mindlessly adhered to!

"Next please," I called from my consulting room and in walked a man with a covered pet-carrying container, accompanied by his, obviously, very excited family.

"Well, what have we got in here then?" I asked.

"It's our new parrot," the children replied in unison. "We have just got him today and we want him checked over to make sure that he's OK." Four little, excited faces peered up at me as I removed the cover and looked inside the carrying cage.

The father then took over the conversation and the kids retreated into the background. It appeared that his main interest was just ensuring that he hadn't been 'done' with his new acquisition and that his money hadn't been wasted! He felt that he had maybe paid 'over the odds' for it because he had bought it from a breeder, and it was supposed to be hand-reared and therefore tame.

I opened the door of the carrier and looked in and sitting quietly on a perch was a most beautiful baby Senegal Parrot which was coloured green with a greyish head and a yellow chest. Quite frequently, birds will either try to escape as soon as a cage door is opened or will retreat to the back of the cage making unhappy, grumbling noises. This gorgeous bird did neither and as I proffered my hand it stepped up onto it and then I gently wrapped it in a towel so that I could hold it and examine it without it flapping its wings or trying to escape or perhaps even trying to bite me!

Five pairs of anxious eyes watched me as I listened to its chest and carried out a thorough examination. The little bird turned out to be as healthy as it was gorgeous and whoever had hand-reared it had done a magnificent job.

"Who would like to listen to his heart beat?" I asked and the four children all beamed and came forward to take their turns using the stethoscope.

"Wow!" was all that they said, obviously well impressed with what they had heard!

"What a lovely little bird you have got. You are very fortunate because not only does he appear healthy but he is incredibly tame as well. I used to keep this type of parrot, but none of them were as tame as this one, in fact they bit me quite regularly! What are you going to call him?"

I was addressing the beaming children at this point and felt that I was developing a good rapport with them. "So, what are you going to call him then?"

Before any of them had a chance to answer, their father announced, "He's called Larsen."

"Larsen!" I repeated, somewhat surprised because I had never met a pet with that name.

"That's an unusual name," I observed. "Well, there must be a story to this name. Why did you call him Larsen?" Then with a sudden flash of inspiration I added, "Ah, so you called him after that American cartoonist that does the 'Far Side' cartoons? So can you spell it for me?"

Mr Lennon looked at me with a blank, uncomprehending, expression. It was quite obvious that he wasn't familiar with the cartoonist's works! As I went to fill out the bird's record details, Mr Lennon replied rather sharply, "Why? It is spelt L A R S S O N of course."

"Oh really?" I replied and continued writing. "Well, there must be story behind giving a bird a name like that. Why did you call him Larsson?"

I didn't look up from what I was doing but I heard Mr Lennon announce in a loud voice. "He's called Larsson because he's called after the best football player in the world!" My heart sank at these words because I knew nothing at all about football and I was quite obviously appearing to be totally ignorant! It sank even further when he added, "And what's more he plays for the best football team in the world!"

As I looked up, I innocently asked, "So, what team is that then?" It was at that exact moment that I saw Mr Lennon drawing himself up to his full 5 feet 4 inches, puffing out his chest as he did so, and with great emphasis, he spat out the words, "Why Celtic, of course!"

At that exact moment, I noticed that all his kids were dressed in green and white tee shirts and he had a similarly coloured scarf wrapped around his neck. What other colour of bird could they possibly have bought but a green and yellow one! It was then quite obvious to me that they certainly would not have countenanced purchasing a Blue Fronted Amazon or even a blue coloured Budgerigar!

I've made a bit of a fool of myself here, I mused, so I thought that I would defuse, what had become a somewhat tense atmosphere by saying something both witty and stupid! I would just 'pull his leg' a little, I thought.

My 'witty' reply of, "Oh! I thought that you were going to say a decent team like…'Airdrie'!" almost caused an apoplectic explosion and I thought for a minute that he was going to hit me!

It is quite obviously not a wise course of action to even attempt to joke about the prowess of some peoples' football teams!

With a scarlet face and the proverbial 'steam coming out his ears', he swept up the parrot in its case and rapidly shepherded his slightly bemused brood out of the consulting room. Moral learned, don't even think about teasing folks about football!

Names of pets can be quite interesting and there is usually a story about the more unusual ones. But I have learned over the years that it can be somewhat of a minefield if one enquires about the reasons for a name or even worse if one tries to second-guess the reason!

I can well remember a little old lady who brought her much loved Gloster canary to see me. Now, for those of you who aren't familiar with this breed, they have a little crown of feathers, that lie flat on the top of their heads and they peer out from under this feathery fringe. So, as usual, I chatted to the lady about her cute little bird and asked her various questions about it, such as where she obtained it and what its name was etc.

"He is called John Paul," she proudly announced and to which, hoping to show the breadth of my musical knowledge, I replied, "Oh, so you are a Beatles fan then?" It was quite obvious to me that there was a connection between the canary's fringed hairstyle and the famous pop group. "Good choice of name, he just looks like the Beatles used to look."

With a shocked look she retorted, "Absolutely not! He's called after His Holiness, of course, our Pope!"

So, I was wrong again but couldn't help thinking that even 'His Holiness' probably wasn't aware that he had the honour of having a little Scottish canary called after him!

Why would anybody call a female, black cat 'Lenin'? Well, that one belonged to a rabid Marxist, who obviously wasn't as educated in the sex of cats as he was in politics! It wasn't even a 'red' male cat! When I asked the owner why 'she' was called Lenin, the client told me that it had belonged to her brother who, in his youth was obsessed with Lenin and so he called his cat after his hero! However, he moved to a city, became a successful businessman and capitalist and so he then left the cat with his sister because 'Lenin' was an embarrassment in front of his new circle of capitalist friends!

The old adage about animals looking like their owners does often have some truth to it. But what is often more remarkable is how the animals often reflect the character of their names!

Satan, the only animal that I have met with that name, was a virtually un-handleable, spitting, clawing, biting demon of a black cat that I never looked forward to seeing! Apparently, he was perfectly behaved at home as long as you didn't interfere with him, but then he would attack with all four sets of claws and his teeth, simultaneously and with such ferocity that he could have shamed a Serengeti Lion! When his life had run its course and he had passed on, his owner then appeared with another cute little black kitten. I felt considerable relief that I didn't have to deal with the satanic behaviour of this kitten's predecessor anymore and asked what she was calling this one.

"He's called 'Fury'!" she said with a wry smile. Fury certainly grew into his name and ended up being even more unsociable and aggressive than Satan! It pays to think carefully when naming a pet!

Some animals have names that suit them such as Spot or Patch or Midget, or even big dogs called Tyson or Bruno after famous boxers. Others can be pretty randomly chosen, and many have human names like George, Betty, Alfie or similar. I will never forget attending a Jack Russell terrier bitch that was having trouble whelping. As, is very often the case, this little bitch was attempting to produce her pups at night, a not uncommon time to give birth.

Her abdomen was relatively enormous compared to the rest of her and it was quite likely that she was going to give birth to a considerable number of puppies. I examined her and after a little bit of digital manipulation, and not a little difficulty, managed to extricate the first pup which was fairly large and had been pretty stuck in the birth canal. It had been there for some time and despite the bitch's best efforts to expel it she had been unsuccessful.

There was a reasonable chance that the pup might have died en-route due to the amount of time it had been stuck. However, it still had a faint heartbeat when it was finally born and with a lot of effort, I managed to get it to eventually breathe on its own. A little cry from it was the best sound ever, as it became aware of, and began to object to, my ministrations.

"Oh, thank you so much son!" said the owner. "I am so extremely grateful to you because I really thought that it would be dead. That's really 'braw', I think we will call it Patch. Do you think that she will manage the rest alright now?"

"Well, I will give her an injection to start her womb contracting again and we will need to wait and see. Hopefully having produced that first big puppy she should manage the rest OK. If she hasn't produced one in half an hour, then give me a call."

Of course, the inevitable happened and in about 45 minutes another call came in requesting another visit. Once again, I had to manipulate a stuck pup and bring it into the world.

"Oh, thank you that is great," the owner said. "We will call this one Spot." The same events were repeated again and again over the next two and a half hours with each pup getting the same declaration of, "Oh! That's good. We will call this one Nipper," etc., until the sixth and final pup appeared. At this point, the owner had obviously run out of names since she had named the previous pups, Spot, Patch, Nipper, Trixie and Benji and she said, "What's your name son?" When I told her, her response was, "Oh my goodness, we cannot cry (call) him that. We will just call him Gyp!"

As far as I am aware, I have only had one animal named after me but even then, they used my surname!

One of the more intriguing names was that of a cat called 'Sexybot'! I saw the name come up on the waiting room list on my computer screen and really didn't think that it could actually be true!

I'm going to have a little bit of fun here when I call the owner in for her consultation! I thought to myself. So, I walked to the waiting room and as I did so I called out, "Sexybot please." Just as I said it, I noticed that the waiting room was absolutely full of people who were waiting to be seen and a lady wearing tight trousers arose from her chair and proceeded to wiggle her way towards me while carrying her cat.

I immediately realised that, from the expressions on the faces of the men in the waiting room, that she did, indeed, have a sexy bot, and furthermore I could tell that they thought I must know her quite well! I hasten to add that I had never met her nor the cat before but I certainly did get to know her quite well thereafter! They were both lovely and it was a sad day when they moved away from the area.

Although the naming of animals is always an intriguing subject, it is certainly not a wise procedure to make comments about them, as I learned on one occasion.

The most beautiful, most pretty, German Shepherd puppy that I had ever seen was gently placed on the consulting room table by her adoring owners; namely Mum, Dad and their 10-year-old daughter.

"My goodness, isn't she just absolutely gorgeous?" I said. "Do you have a name for her yet?"

"Yes," Mum replied, whilst beaming with pride. "We are going to call her…Primrose."

I must admit to being a bit surprised because that was certainly an unusual name for a German Shepherd bitch! However, I tried not to show it and casually remarked, "Primrose? Now that is a different name for a Shepherd!"

"Yes, we thought so too," replied the mother. "We wanted a name that was a bit different to the usual ones."

"Well, yes, Primrose is certainly a different name. I don't think that I have met a dog called Primrose before." Then for some stupid reason added. "Well at least you didn't call her something really common like Tara or Tanya like everyone else does!"

"That's what our last two dogs were called!" wailed the young girl somewhat indignantly!

Oh dear! Perhaps I shouldn't have said anything!

Children can be really fun to have at a consultation with their pets but there are some who are totally out of control and whose parents just let them run wild. Opening drawers, trying to put their hand into the 'sharps' bins or grabbing hold of the diagnostic kit and its rechargeable handles, were not uncommon. On one occasion, a youngster got hold of my stethoscope ear piece and pulled it out of one of my ears, only to then let go and let if forcefully spring back into my ear. Painful indeed! Did mother reprimand him? Not at all! Suffice to say that when she needed to go out the room for something that she had left in her car, she found him standing quietly in the corner when she returned!

Children can always be relied upon to tell the truth, sometimes embarrassing their parents and sometimes embarrassing the vet!

I will never forget a lady, together with her little daughter of probably 5 or 6 years of age, bringing in their wire-haired Pointer to check to see whether she was pregnant or not. There was great excitement about the bitch being possibly pregnant for the first time but this was tempered by some doubt since she didn't look pregnant: hence the visit. After a manual palpation of her abdomen, I was able to relay to them the happy news that she was, indeed, pregnant.

"Is she really?" was the excited question from her owner, "Wow! That is really good because we were beginning to think that the mating had not been successful. She really hasn't put any weight on so do you think she's going to have many pups?"

After ascertaining how long it was since the mating, I replied that I didn't think she would be having too many pups because her womb wasn't very large. After continued pressure from the owner, I ventured to tell her that five would be the probable number, but at the same time stressing to her how it was impossible to be certain. Mother and daughter virtually danced out of the consulting room, full of joy and excitement!

Approximately, five weeks later I noticed that my next appointment was to check over some newborn pups. In waltzed the Pointer owner carrying a large basket which was covered with a blanket and who was being followed by her little daughter who was skipping and jumping.

"Did everything go OK with the whelping?" I asked.

"Yes! Absolutely fine," was the response. "She did really well and didn't need any help from us. It took a little while until she was finished though. Could you check her over too and make sure there are no more pups left?"

"Sure, we can do that if you bring her in after we have checked the pups over. How many did she have in the end then?" I asked as I removed the cover from the basket.

"Ten!" was the answer.

"Oh, my goodness! Ten?" I asked.

A small voice piped up from the 5-year-old who was standing with hands on hips and swaying cockily from side to side. "And somebody told us she was only having five!"

Ha, ha! Out of the mouths of babes! We had a good laugh about it though and all was well!

My next episode involving a comment from a small child wasn't in such pleasant circumstances.

A 12-week-old Yellow Labrador was placed on the consulting room table by an anxious looking man who was accompanied by his small daughter; a shy little girl aged about 5 or 6 years of age.

The little dog looked pretty miserable as it sat there holding up its right front leg.

"He won't use his front leg," the man informed me.

I examined the pup who had a very painful elbow and which was, to me at least, quite obviously fractured.

"Is it bad?" enquired the owner.

"Yes, it's serious," I replied. "He has fractured the end of his humerus."

The expression on the man's face changed from one of concern to a decided grimace. He winced as he then asked, "Is it fixable?"

"Yes, it is fixable but he will need an operation to screw the bone fragments back together."

"Oh dear! An operation! I don't think we will bother! He's not been with us long and I'm not going to be spending money on him. Anyway, you can't guarantee that he will be OK, can you?"

"Yes, he will need an operation if he is to walk again and no, I can't guarantee the result, but these fractures do usually heal fairly well."

His response was somewhat surprising. "I just want him put to sleep. I'd rather get another new pup."

I must admit that I was totally taken aback by this statement and I began to take a dislike to this man and his attitude and so I asked him how the pup had sustained his injury.

"He fell down the back steps into the garden," was his curt reply.

"Oh no, he didn't!" said a small voice from behind him. "He broke his leg when you kicked him out the back door after he had wet the kitchen floor!"

Well, the man's face was a picture! The truth had been told and I suspect that he knew that he was in danger of getting prosecuted!

"Er, well, I think we will get his leg fixed after all. Maybe that would be the best course of action!"

Shamed by a child! The pup got its operation and it recovered well but it wasn't the father who returned with it for its check-ups! He sent his wife!